Fractured Fairy Tales

Puppet Plays & Patterns

Marilyn Lohnes

UpstartBooks

Fort Atkinson, Wisconsin

Published by **UpstartBooks**
W5527 Highway 106
P.O. Box 800
Fort Atkinson, Wisconsin 53538-0800
1-800-448-4887

The paper used in this publication meets the minimum requirements of American National Standard for Information Science — Permanence of Paper for Printed Library Material. ANSI/NISO Z39.48-1992.

Library of Congress Cataloging-in-Publication Data
Lohnes, Marilyn, 1963-
    Fractured fairy tales : puppet plays & patterns / Marilyn Lohnes.
        p. cm.
Includes bibliographical references.
    ISBN 1-57950-073-0 (alk. paper)
 1. Puppet plays, American. 2. Puppet making. 3. Puppet theater. I. Title.
    PN1980 .L64 2002
    812'.6–dc21
                                            2002012882

Contents

Introduction

In these days of video games, satellite television, and Pentium computers, one might think that an ancient and simple method of entertainment such as puppetry would be long dead. Not so. In fact, quite the opposite is true. Puppetry has never died and recently, its art has experienced a unique revival. It continues to entertain children of all ages. It encourages children to express themselves creatively and to develop their imagination. Watch the faces of children during a puppet presentation and you will know exactly what I mean. As the puppet, an inanimate object, is brought to life with imagination, the children laugh and point, carry on a lively conversation with the puppet, or even warn the character of impending danger.

In more recent years, however, puppetry has taken on an additional and very important role. Not only do puppets entertain—they educate. For the younger child they can foster language development. For the older child they can teach lessons and impart values; thus they become an invaluable method of instruction and communication. Both schools and church groups are becoming more involved in puppetry as an entertaining and exciting way of teaching children. Lessons learned in this way are more often remembered over a longer period of time.

The History of Puppetry

Puppetry is an ancient art that has survived for thousands of years. Records from the fifth century B.C. describe religious ceremonies in Egypt involving puppets. The records suggest that puppetry was not a new phenomenon. In ancient Egypt, long before the pyramids were built, and also in Greece and Rome, puppets were incorporated into religious festivals. At these times, puppets were exclusively for adult audiences. Puppets were sacred objects and were often buried in tombs of important people. In modern archaeological excavations Egyptian clay marionettes have been discovered. In another part of the world, the natives of Mexico were also using puppets in their religious ceremonies. Diaries from the Cortez expedition refer to the use of puppets in Indian ceremonies.

In the Middle East, puppetry was used to express the folklore of India, Persia, Burma, and Turkey. Marionettes became popular there as well as in France, Italy, and Spain, and puppeteers were honored professionals. The Chinese and Japanese were also familiar with puppetry. Japanese puppeteers constructed elaborate marionettes and, in the eighteenth century, wrote for the national puppet theater. The Chinese, along with the Turks, experimented with shadow puppets. To this day, Chinese cultural groups still present shadow plays of well-known stories such as *The Nightingale* and *The Emperor's New Clothes.*

Puppets were used in the early Christian churches to tell religious stories. Their popularity as religious characters was not long-lived, as arguments abounded as to whether God should be reduced to a puppet. Consequently, puppeteers returned to street performances of popular stories and folklore. In the Middle Ages, King Arthur's court was often entertained by troubadours and puppeteers. Punch and Judy were immortalized during that time.

Puppetry in the United States and Canada took a little longer to be popularized. Although immigrants from England, France, Germany, and Italy brought puppets and puppetry skills with them, the concept was not an instant success. It was not until the advent of television that these small characters became widely known to Americans. Television shows such as *Kukla, Fran and Ollie* in the United States, and *Mr. Dressup* and *The Friendly Giant* in Canada, created puppet characters that became household names. Later came *Sesame Street* and the resulting birth of the Muppets®. All of this led to the explosion of puppetry in North America.

Today, puppetry is used for entertainment at public libraries and day cares, for educational purposes at schools and churches, and for counseling at hospitals and clinics. As we continue to develop and refine puppets, we continue to learn new things about puppets and puppetry. As we have learned from puppeteers before us, so too will future puppeteers learn from us. Presentation methods may differ, as may the puppets themselves, but in itself the art of puppetry will live on. Long live the puppet! Long live the puppeteer!

Types of Puppets

Quite simply, a puppet is an inanimate object, constructed of wood, cloth, plastic, cardboard, papier-mâché, or any other type of material, brought to life and personified by the puppeteer. The puppet does not need to look like a human being, rather it must act like one. This is the puppeteer's job and it will be discussed later.

The Marionette

Marionettes are generally fashioned from wood and resemble a human body. Body joints (ankles, knees, etc.) are connected by movable hinges. String is attached to various parts of the body, but most commonly to the arms, legs, and head, and it allows the puppeteer to create very lifelike movements. Although marionettes are renowned as an artistic and sophisticated method of puppetry, they are difficult to manipulate, especially for the beginner. For the inexperienced marionette operator, the performance can be frustrating, as the puppet may not move in the intended fashion, and the operation strings may tangle or break.

Shadow Puppets

Similar to the marionette, but less sophisticated, is the shadow puppet. Shadow puppets are generally flat characters created from heavy paper or cardboard. Again, the characters are hinged, thus allowing the puppets to move freely, and rods are used to operate the gross movements. The figures are placed against a thin fabric panel, and a bright light is shone behind the screen. The result is that the audience sees a clear silhouette or shadow of a puppet. Although these puppets are quite simple to produce, they are not always simple to present.

Stick Puppets

Like most puppets, stick puppets vary in their complexity. A stick puppet can be as simple as a Styrofoam ball head attached to a stick, or a two-dimensional picture attached to a stick, or as complicated as a two-stick process whereby one stick supports the puppet's head and body and the other stick becomes an arm and hand. Puppets can also be created using wooden spoons. Spoon puppets are easy to create and manipulate, but the puppeteer is restricted to very simple movements when using them.

Hand Puppets

Hand puppets are by far the most common type of puppet. They are relatively simple to create and readily available to purchase for those who are not inclined to make their own. With a hand puppet, the puppeteer's hand is placed directly inside the puppet. Different fingers control the head and arms of the puppet. In addition to moving their head and arms, these puppets can pick up or manipulate props. The puppet becomes an extension of the puppeteer's own hand, thus making movements with the puppet relatively natural. I recommend this type of puppet, particularly for the beginning puppeteer.

Mouth Puppets

(Muppet® type)

Mouth puppets are my favorite type of puppet. They appear more lifelike than their counterparts (although this is not necessarily important to the child).

Mouth puppets are distinguished from other puppets in that they have movable mouths, thus allowing the puppets to talk more realistically. The puppeteer inserts his thumb into the lower jaw of the puppet and the other fingers operate the upper jaw. If the mouth puppet also has a body and arms, the puppeteer must decide what to do with the arms. A beginner might choose to simply leave the arms hanging to the side of the puppet. A second option is to tie some fishing line or invisible thread to both the wrist and the neck of the puppet. Consequently, any large movement by the puppet would result in smaller movements of the arms. The third option is to use rods with the puppet. Rods fastened to the wrists are used to manipulate the hands and arms of a mouth puppet. It takes practice to manipulate the hands in this fashion, but once the method has been mastered, the results are extremely rewarding.

Manipulation
Giving Life to Your Puppets

A puppet is nothing more than a puppet until the puppeteer gives it life. With the help of the puppeteer's hand it can jump, run, bow, sneeze, or do just about anything a person can.

Holding a Hand Puppet

Although there are several ways to hold a hand puppet, my preferred method is to have the thumb and baby finger as the arms, and the index finger as the neck. The other two fingers are simply folded down. In this position the hand is more relaxed. The arms can spread the entire breadth of the body, and the wrist and neck joint are quick to manipulate.

There are three basic movements in hand puppetry. The first, done by moving the fingers, corresponds to puppet movements of the hands and head. The second, done by moving the wrist, corresponds to puppet movements of the waist. The third, done by moving the arm, corresponds to puppet movements as a whole unit, i.e., walking, running, jumping.

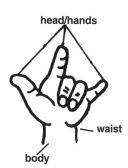

Holding a Mouth Puppet

To manipulate a mouth puppet, slide the thumb into the lower jaw of the puppet. The remaining fingers go into the upper jaw. The mouth is opened and closed by moving the fingers. The four fingers in the puppet's upper jaw stay together, while the thumb is lowered and raised to create a moving mouth. The mouth may open and close for each syllable spoken, for each stressed syllable, or for each word. The mouth must fully open and close in speech, as a half-opened mouth looks awkward. Another trick in speaking with a mouth puppet is to push the hand slightly forward on the syllables emphasized.

Mouth puppetry has three basic movements as well. The fingers correspond to mouth movements and facial expressions, the wrist corresponds to neck and head movements, and the arm corresponds to whole unit movements such as walking and running.

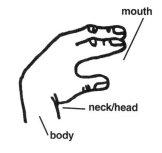

Eye Contact

Eye contact gives the puppet the illusion of life. The audience will be looking where the puppets are looking, so be sure to plan the direction of the puppets. If one puppet is talking and the other puppet is looking at him, the puppets must be facing each other. Similarly, if the puppet is speaking to the audience, it must be looking at the audience. When looking at the audience, make sure the puppet is looking down, as the audience is generally seated on the floor.

With mouth puppets there is a natural tendency to hold the hand upward toward the ceiling. This makes the puppet look as if it were staring at the sky. Be sure to bend the wrist downward. It may take some practice to remember to do this.

Position of Puppet's Hands

Unless the puppeteer has remarkable flexibility in both the baby finger and the thumb, it is impossible for a hand puppet to hold its hands downward as though resting at the sides. For this reason, it is necessary to find another position that is both comfortable for the puppeteer and natural in appearance for the puppet. The arms may be held straight out, though I find this a little awkward in appearance. The average person does not stand with their arms outstretched for lengthy periods of time. My preferred method is to rest the arms against the puppet's middle by folding both the thumb and the baby finger in. The puppet can manipulate props by simply reaching out and holding the prop with the thumb and baby finger.

Quite the opposite of the hand puppet is the mouth puppet. Since the hands of most mouth puppets are not functional, they tend to hang loosely at the sides of the puppet. This makes for a relaxed pose, but creates problems when hands are needed. In the case of animal puppets, the puppeteer may use the mouth to pick up or manipulate props. On a long-necked mouth puppet such as a snake, the fingers, wrist and arm must coordinate their movements to create a slithering creature that can chew or spit out props. Mouth puppets that resemble people should not use their mouth to manipulate props, as it would appear very unnatural. Rods may be attached to the hands of these puppets to allow movement of the hands, but this still does not allow picking up props, etc. Backdrops work much better than stage props for mouth puppets, and generally give the same impression.

Entering and Exiting Stage

The entrance and exit of a puppet may depend largely upon its character. For example, the snake in "Jungle Jack and the Vinestalk" might slowly slither onstage, pause, then continue, while the rabbit in "Little Red Racing Heart" might suddenly pop onstage, race across the opening, and quickly depart. The ghost in "The Princess and the Pumpkin" might slowly sway onstage from side to side, while the aliens in "Zip Van Blinkle" might simply pop straight up. For those puppets without a defined personality, the basic entrance is tiered, meaning the puppet appears to be coming up a flight of stairs onto the stage. When walking, the puppet turns slightly from side to side. For the hand puppet, the movement is done with the wrist to create waist movement, while the movement for the mouth puppet involves a more general arm movement in which the hand sways from side to side over the elbow. Exiting is done in the same way, except the puppet appears to be walking down a flight of stairs and offstage.

Basic Movements and Actions

A puppet is expected to act out its story, not only through speech, but also through actions. If the puppet is angry it might jump up and down, or if it is unhappy it might slump over. The following is a list of some basic puppet actions and suggestions on how to accomplish the movement.

Snoring: For hand puppets, bend the waist of the puppet down, then with slow, jerking motions raise it up. For mouth puppets, open the mouth extremely wide, then close the mouth with slow, jerking motions.

Sneezing: For hand puppets, arch the body backwards, then as the sneeze lets go, bend the puppet at the waist. For mouth puppets, open the mouth wide, arch the head backwards, and then quickly close the mouth and point the head forward.

Crying: This can be similar to sneezing, but with more jerking motions as the puppet sobs.

Nodding Yes: For hand puppets, wave the index finger slowly forward, then to an upright position.

For mouth puppets, bend the wrist slowly to the floor, then back to eye-level position.

Nodding No: For hand puppets, the whole body must turn from side to side, as the head cannot do this on its own. Using the wrist, move the puppet slowly right then left. For mouth puppets, turn the wrist from side to side to make the puppet's head nod no.

Demonstrating Self: For hand puppets, draw the thumb or baby finger in to the puppet's middle to indicate pointing to self. For mouth puppets, raise the head upward and to one side, as though striking an arrogant pose.

Excitement: For hand puppets, clap the hands by bringing thumb and index finger together. For mouth puppets, bounce puppet up and down with arm and open puppet's mouth as if to say "Hooray!"

Thinking: For hand puppets, rub the puppet head with one hand by moving either the thumb or the baby finger. For mouth puppets, have puppet stare off to side with a slightly upward look. This can be done by gently twisting the wrist. The puppet can also sigh by opening and closing the mouth.

Pointing: For hand puppets, simply point by raising one of the puppet's hands in the appropriate direction. For mouth puppets, stretch the neck and head of the puppet forward in the appropriate direction.

Puppet Voices

Once you have practiced basic movements and manipulation and have given life to your puppet, you must decide what you want your puppet to sound like. Puppets need voices of their own, distinct from human voices so that the audience identifies with the puppet, not with the human who is manipulating the puppet.

Creating voices for puppets is really not all that difficult. Simply modify your human voice to become puppet voices. Begin with your own range of voice. Humans have high-pitched voices (which might show excitement), natural speaking voices, and low or deep-throated voices (which might show disapproval or anger). Between these ranges are an infinite number of other voices, pitches, and tones. Try experimenting with your voice by tape recording several samples of it in different ranges.

The next step in determining a puppet voice is matching the size of the puppet to the volume of the voice. A lion puppet, for example, might have a loud, growling voice, whereas a mouse would have a small, soft, squeaking voice. This is important, as the audience must identify with each puppet separately. A lion and a mouse who spoke similarly would be difficult for the audience to distinguish.

Once range and volume are established, the puppeteer must provide character to the voice. The job of the puppeteer is to convince the audience that the character he or she is presenting is real. There are a number of methods which will accomplish this. One, as mentioned earlier, is to add a tone to the puppet's voice. The lion's voice might be "growly," while the mouse's voice would be "squeaky." The Grandmother's voice might be scratchy, while the silly or dumb puppet might have a slow, sluggish voice. Another method is to use exaggerated alliteration. For example, a sheep puppet might exaggerate the letter "b" to make "baa." The speaking voice might be something like this:

Gee, that's too baaaaad, I'll have to go baaaaack.

Similarly, the cow might reply,

It's mmmmooooost unfortunate, I hope you don't mmmmind.

Another method is to use character identification words, sounds, or actions. For example, a little girl might constantly giggle, while a witch might cackle before each line of speech. Similarly, in action, an elf puppet might jump up and down excitedly before speaking, while a ghost might moan and sway. Try imagining your puppet as a live character. Imagine what its voice would sound like, and then practice that sound with the help of a tape recorder.

Puppet Stages

We have a whole world in which to live. Within it we choose where to live and what to do. Puppets need their own world as well. For them, their world is the stage. Within it they can run, play, and generally behave as a living being would. The opening, or *proscenium,* is the working area for the puppeteer, and is generally seen by the audience as a picture frame in which the puppets perform. The puppets are easily seen, but the puppeteer is hidden from the audience behind the stage, either sitting, kneeling, or standing, depending on the stage. This creates a detachment between the puppet and the puppeteer, making the puppet characters seem more alive to the audience.

The puppet's stage can be as simple or as complicated as you choose to make it. Below are a few examples of each.

Simple Stages

Doorway Stage: For the beginning puppeteer, a doorway stage is an easy way to create a puppet world. Simply stretch a blanket across an open doorway. The blanket should be at a height that is about two inches over the puppeteer's head when the puppeteer is sitting or kneeling. The door frame creates a natural opening in which the puppeteer can perform.

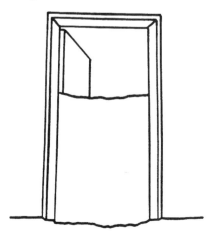

Table Stage: Another simple stage is the table stage. Turn a rectangular table onto its side. Set the table in a suitable place for the puppet show, with the tabletop facing the audience. Drape blankets over the front and sides of the table. An option for a taller stage is to lay the table on top of another table which is standing upright.

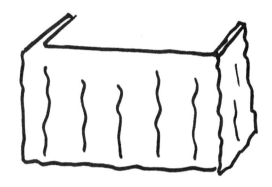

Cardboard Box Stage: A cardboard box from a refrigerator can also make a nice, simple puppet stage. Remove the top and one side of the box, then stand the box on its bottom. Cut an opening for the stage so that the bottom of the opening is approximately two inches above the puppeteer's head when sitting or kneeling.

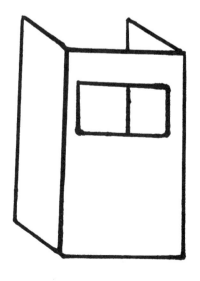

Professional Stages

Wooden Puppet Stage: The wooden stage is made from three ¾–1" plywood panels; two are 42" x 84", while the third is 60" x 84". The panels are securely fastened together at 90° angles to form three sides of a stage with the wide piece being the middle. The fourth side is left open for the puppeteer to enter and exit. Cut an opening 18" x 42" approximately 56" from the floor. A shelf may be bracketed to the lower edge of the opening for a platform for props. A curtain may be added by creating two grooves in the upper part of the side panels that are large enough to insert a dowel. The curtain can be hung over the dowel or threaded through it.

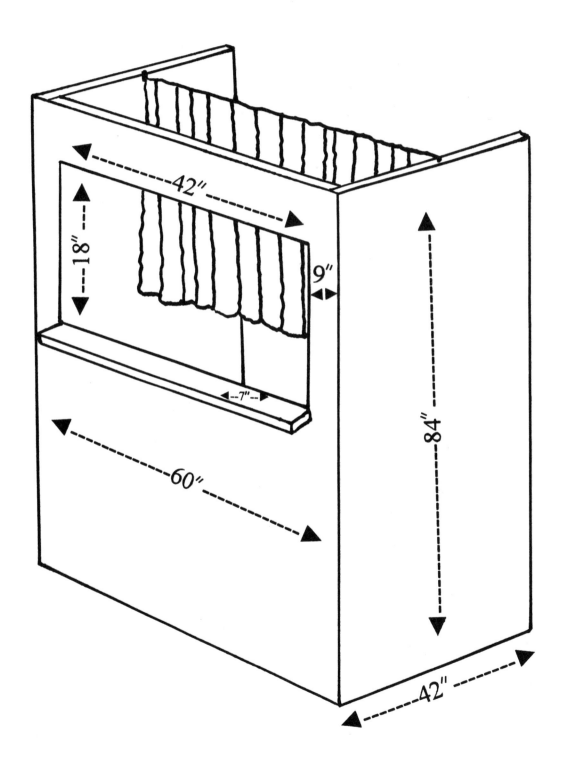

Portable Pipe Puppet Stage: The portable pipe stage is excellent for puppeteers who travel, or for classrooms or libraries that have little storage space. The stage, when unassembled, is light and compact, when assembled, it is large and professional. It has the added benefit of having more than one opening, so puppets can move from level to level to perform. The frame is constructed entirely of plastic piping (any size between ¾" and 2" diameter is fine, but make sure you use the same type throughout the stage) and is covered in a heavy fabric (I prefer velvet). To build it you need:

- 3 pieces of piping 70–72" long
- 2 pieces of piping 54–56" long
- 4 pieces of piping 43–45" long

- 8 pieces of piping 34–36" long
- 2 pieces of piping 14–16" long
- 2 pieces of piping 10–12" long
- 10 90° connectors
- 10 T connectors
- Approximately 15–20 yards of fabric

Assemble the stage as illustrated. Drape fabric or sew panels for front and sides. If you choose to sew the panels, create them as you would make a curtain panel, with the piping being the curtain rod. For front and side, panels should be 1–2" longer than the height of the frame, and two to three times wider to create fullness. For middle and back, panels should be approximately halfway to floor in length, and two to three times wider for fullness.

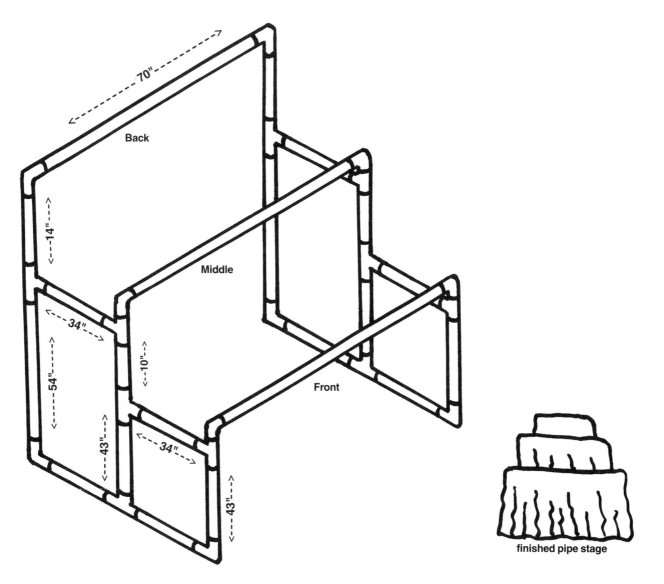

finished pipe stage

Props, Backdrops, and Lighting

With props and scenery it is easy to transform the stage into a forest, house, castle, or any place you want your puppets to be. The audience is transported into a time, place, or mood with just a few props or a simple backdrop. The choice of props or scenery depends largely upon which type of stage you prefer to use, and how simple or professional you want your show to be.

Props

Props are objects other than the puppets which are used in the puppet production. The table stage and the wooden puppet stage lend themselves well to the use of props. In both stages there is a solid surface safe for placing prop items. Generally speaking, props should be made of unbreakable materials. Even with the most experienced puppeteers, objects from the stage occasionally fall off the stage. Props should also be large enough for the audience to see. Props made to scale for the puppet are often too small to be of any practical use, and are not interesting to the audience. Larger, disproportional props are easier for the puppeteer to manipulate, and are comical for the audience.

Hand puppets can place their own props on and off the stage, but the mouth puppets require assistance. In placing props on or off the stage, one should try to show as little of the hand as possible. One suggestion I heard was to use a brightly colored glove to move the props. With a little imagination the glove could be made into a prop puppet, with roly eyes and a felt smile. It could scamper about the stage, adding, removing, and rearranging props. If the puppet show is based on a particular theme, the prop puppet could be dressed accordingly.

Suspended props can be easily manipulated by hanging some fishing line over a dowel which is fastened to the upper part of the stage. In "Jungle Jack and the Vinestalk" a movable vine is used to create the image of Jack climbing the vinestalk. When the vinestalk is lowered, it appears that Jack is at the top of it, while when the vinestalk is raised, Jack appears to be at the bottom of it. A movable reptile is also used for "Triceralocks and the Saber-tooth Bears."

Stick props may be used with any type of stage, regardless of whether a stage platform is present or not. Two-dimensional props can be fastened to sticks and simply held up to the stage. The large valentine prop in "Little Red Racing Hood" would work well as a stick prop.

Backdrops

Scenery is best presented through the use of backdrops. Backdrops are painted pieces of fabric which are hung behind the proscenium, or opening. A number of trees painted on a backdrop will indicate a forest to the audience, while a small house might suggest the puppet is on its way to that particular house. Scenes can be changed in two ways. The scenes can be sewn or taped together and flipped over like a flip chart, or the scenes can be placed on a rod with curtain rings and one scene can simply be slid away when another one is introduced.

Lighting

Generally as long as the room in which the puppet show is being presented is well lit, no special lighting is required. However, some puppeteers prefer to have a light source shining directly onto the puppets from in front of the stage. This can easily be done by clamping a small flood or spotlight to the outside of the puppet stage.

Puppeteers may wish to experiment with colored lights. A green light would enhance a forest or jungle scene, while a blue light might suggest an underwater scene. "Little Red Racing Heart" might be presented using a red light for a valentine mood, while "Little Green O'Glenn and the Lazy Leprechauns" might be presented with a green light to suggest St. Patrick's Day.

Sound and Special Effects

Music

Most puppet shows are enhanced with the use of music. Music can announce the beginning of a puppet show, changes in scenes, particular moods or events, and the finale. Puppet shows with a particular theme require music related to that theme. For example, I open "Triceralocks and the Sabertooth Bears" with a song called "Dinosaur Dance" *(Rhinoceros Tap: And 14 Other Seriously Silly Songs)*. It is strongly advised, particularly in Canada, to seek out the current copyright legislation for public performances of music. It may be necessary to purchase a background music license.

Taped Shows

As the puppeteer you must decide whether you will be performing live, or whether you will be taping the puppet show. A live show provides the performer with more control over the production and opportunities to interact with the audience. Taped shows, however, are convenient in that all script, sound effects, and music are incorporated into the recording. The puppeteer need do nothing more than press the "play" button and begin performing. Should you elect to tape your puppet show, be prepared to have several practice runs to match the script with the puppet's movements and speaking.

Special Effects

A puppet show is long remembered by its audience if a few special effects have been slipped in the show. Here are a few simple suggestions to make your puppet show more exciting:

Sound Effects

- **Thunder:** rattle disposable aluminum pie plates
- **Rain:** whirl small marbles in a disposable aluminum pie plate
- **Running Water:** pour water from a mason jar into larger jar or bucket
- **Wind:** blow across an empty soda bottle
- **Fire:** crumple a sheet of paper
- **Heavy Footsteps:** turn a bucket upside down behind stage and stamp on the bucket
- **Galloping Horse:** pat knees quickly
- **Tinkling Sounds:** jingle car keys

Special Effects

- **Smoke:** squeeze baby powder bottle
- **Lightning:** quickly turn light on and off
- **Magic Wand:** party sparkler
- **Ice:** plastic wrap
- **Icicles:** icicle lights
- **Snow:** white confetti

The Plays

This book contains 10 puppet plays, all loosely based on well-known fairy tales. They represent different themes, environments, and holidays. The presentation time of each show ranges from 10 to 20 minutes, depending on factors such as the length of musical interludes, the duration of chase scenes, etc. The plays are suitable for both preschool and school-age audiences. Preschool children will enjoy the humor and action of the shows, while the older children will identify with the original fairy tales and will appreciate some of the more subtle humor. Classrooms may choose to present a puppet performance to a younger audience as part of a theater arts curriculum, or teachers and librarians may produce a more elaborate presentation of the show for a general or kindergarten audience.

Coordinators should select a puppet script that is suitable in its timing and theme. Upon selection of a script, the coordinator needs to determine how many puppeteers are necessary. All of the shows can be performed with two puppeteers for library presentation (though some are more difficult this way) but classroom presentations might entail one puppet and character per child. Patterns for some of the props are included, while other props will require some innovation and thought. With a little preparation, the puppet script can be transformed into a lively and entertaining performance.

The Three Little Fishies and the Big, Bad Shark

An Underwater Twist on "The Three Little Pigs"

■_■_■_■_■_■_■_■_■_■_■_■_■_■_■_■_■

Number of Puppets: 4

- 1st Fish
- 2nd Fish
- 3rd Fish
- Shark

Playing Time: 10 minutes

Props:

- House of seaweed (pattern, p. 23)
- House of shells (pattern, p. 24)
- House of rocks (pattern, p. 25)
- Tin can with bow

Setting: Underwater scene

Lighting: No special effects

Music: Any children's music about water, or classical with tide sounds

Scene 1

Action:	*Music (approx. 20 seconds). One by one the fishies arrive onstage.*
1st Fish:	Oh, oh, wasn't it awful to see mother crying like that?
2nd Fish:	Well, it was really sad news. Mother is so poor that she can't take care of us anymore.
3rd Fish:	I hope you were listening carefully to what Mother told us about going off on our own. She said we must build our own separate homes, where we will be safe and secure from that big, bad shark who lives in the sea.
1st Fish:	Ah, shark, smark. I'm not afraid of that toothy troublemaker.
2nd Fish:	Me either. He doesn't scare me. Who's afraid of the big, bad shark?
1st Fish/2nd Fish:	*(Dancing and singing.)* Who's afraid of the big, bad shark …
3rd Fish:	You two should be afraid of the shark. After all, he *does* eat fish.
1st Fish:	Nah, don't be such a worry wartfish.
2nd Fish:	Yeah, we can look after ourselves.

3rd Fish:	Remember, you must promise to build yourselves good strong houses so the shark won't be able to get inside and have you for dinner.
1st Fish:	You're not my mother. You don't have to worry about me. I'll just follow the path to the left. *(1st Fish exits.)*
2nd Fish:	And me? I can stand on my own two fins. I'll take the path to the right. I'm positive that's the best one. *(2nd Fish exits.)*
3rd Fish:	I won't forget you, Mother. I will build myself a good, strong home. And I'll follow that path there—the straight and narrow one. *(3rd Fish exits.)*
Shark:	*(Enters.)* Did I just see three little fishies go by? YUMMMEE! Tuna casserole … fish and chips … poached salmon … *(Shark exits while talking.)*

Scene 2

Action:	*A water scene filled with seaweed. Music (approx. 15 seconds). Enter 1st Fish.*
1st Fish:	This looks like a good place to settle down. There's plenty of food nearby, and I won't even have to build a real house. I'll just hollow out a hole in this seaweed and live inside. That won't take any work at all. *(Put seaweed house onstage.)* There! Instant housing! Oh, such a smart fish I am. Now, I'll just go inside and take a nap. *(Fish goes behind house.)*
Shark:	*(Enters suddenly, sniffs.)* Mmmm. I smell something GOOOOOD. Boys and girls, is it chicken I smell? No—rabbit? No—fish? *(Sniffs again.)* Yes, it's definitely fish. *(Knocks on door.)* Little fish, little fish, let me come in!
1st Fish:	OOOOOH, not by the scales on my finny, fin, fin.
Shark:	Then I'll splash, and I'll thrash, and I'll smash your house down! *(Shark begins to thrash; house falls down.)*
1st Fish:	Oh no! My house! Where's my house? Where's my MOOOMMMY!
Shark:	Stop, my little fish stick! I'll get you yet! *(Chase ensues on stage; fish escapes and exits stage.)* Rats! He got away! *(Shark exits.)*

Scene 3

Action:	*Sea setting with sea shells on stage. Music (approx. 15 seconds). Enter 2nd Fish.*
2nd Fish:	I must have swum for ages and I still haven't found a deserted house to live in. *(Heavy sigh.)* I guess I'll have to build my own house after all. Let me see … oh, my, there are lots of shells around here. I'll just build a house out of them.

(Put shell house on stage.) There! What do you think, boys and girls? *(Taps on house and it nearly falls over.)* I'm sure this will be just fine. *(Yawns.)* Boy, this house-making is no fun at all. I think I'll just go inside for a nap now. *(Fish goes behind house.)*

Shark: *(Enters quickly, sniffing.)* Ahhh, maybe this is my lucky day after all. *(Sniffs around some more.)* YES SIR, I see fish and chips for supper. *(Knocks on door.)* Little fish, little fish, let me come in!

2nd Fish: OOOOOH, not by the scales on my finny, fin, fin.

Shark: Then I'll splash, and I'll thrash and I'll smash your house down! *(Shark begins to thrash; house falls down.)*

2nd Fish: OOOOOH, I don't want to be fish sticks, I don't want to be fish sticks! *(Chase ensues on stage; fish escapes and exits stage.)*

Shark: Rats! He got away! Those little haddocks can sure swim fast! *(Shark exits.)*

Scene 4

Action: *Sea setting with rocks on stage. Music (approx. 15 seconds). Enter 3rd Fish.*

3rd Fish: Gosh, I wonder how my brothers are getting along. I hope they listened and built themselves safe homes. Well, I guess I should start my home. Now, let's see. What can I use to build a good strong home? Boys and girls, do you see anything strong that I could make a house with? Rocks? Why, yes! Rocks would make a wonderfully strong home. And there are plenty of rocks on the bottom of the sea.

(Singing.)
I'll use these fine stones
to build me a home
'cause I promised my mother
that I'd never roam.
There's a big, bad shark
who'll eat me up fast
unless I build a house
that will last and last and last.

(Put stone house on stage.) My goodness, these rocks are heavy, but a good strong house is worth all the work. There! A shark-proof house. Now I'll just go inside and finish up the kitchen.

Shark: *(Enters quickly, sniffing.)* I smell fish stew, and this time I'm not going to let it get away! *(Knocks on door.)* Little fish, little fish, let me come in!

3rd Fish:	NO SIR! Not by the scales on my finny, fin, fin.
Shark:	Then I'll splash, and I'll thrash and I'll smash your house down! *(Shark begins to thrash; house does not move.)* Hmmm, maybe I'll have to try chomping your house down! *(Shark begins to chew at house.)* OOOOOH, my teeth!
3rd Fish:	*(Laughing.)* Go ahead, Mr. Shark. You'll break every tooth before you chew this house down!
Shark:	Not so fast, my handsome herring! I haven't really tried yet! I'll thrash *and* I'll chew! *(Shark splashes around and chews at house.)* OOOOOH my poor teeth! Oooooh, my sore fins!
3rd Fish:	*(Giggles and sings.)* Who's afraid of the big, bad shark ...
Shark:	Well, I'm not finished yet. Boys and girls, what do you think I should do? Do you think there's a window in the back I can swim in? I'll try! *(Exits.)*
3rd Fish:	Oh, oh, I'd better do something about that shark. I'll just bring out my canning supplies and ... *(Shark dives into house; loud struggle ensues; large can with bow is placed on stage.)* There! Shark in a can! Now when my little brothers come to visit, I can serve sandwiches! *(Exit, singing.)* Who's afraid of the big, bad shark ...

(Music.)

■ ▪ ■ ▪ ■ ▪ ■ ▪ ■ ▪ ■ ▪ ■ ▪ ■ ▪ ■ ▪ ■ ▪ ■ ▪ ■ ▪ ■ ▪ ■ ▪ ■ ▪ ■ ▪ ■ ▪

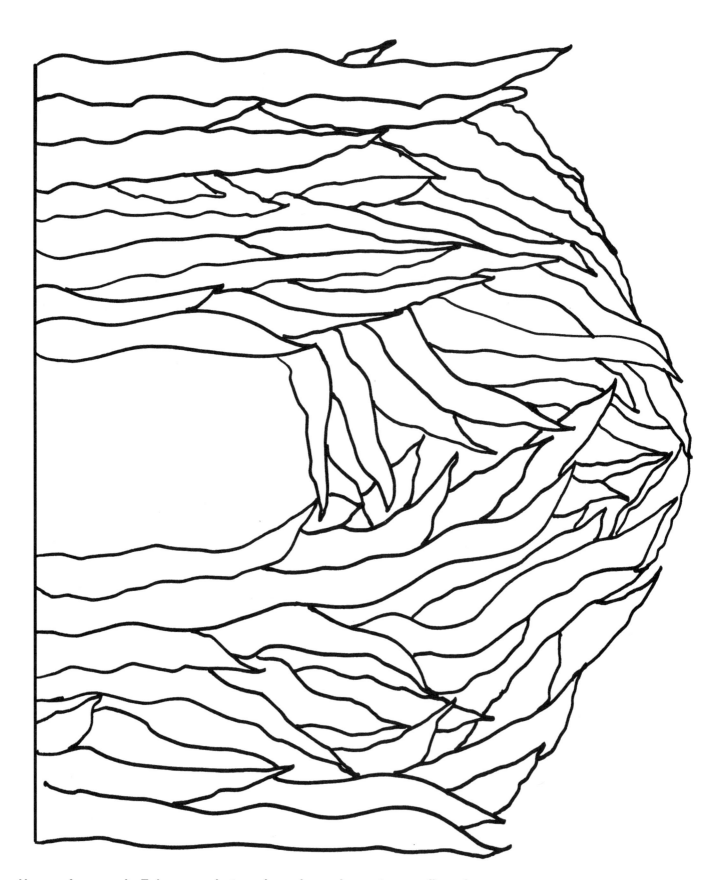

House of seaweed—Enlarge on photocopier, color, and mount on cardboard.

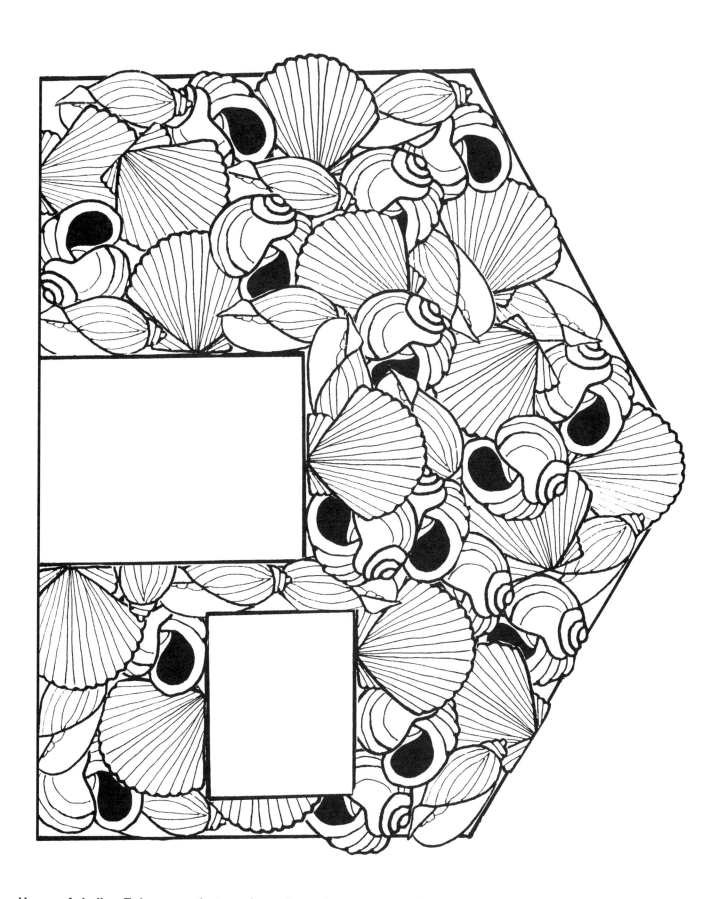

House of shells—Enlarge on photocopier, color, and mount on cardboard.

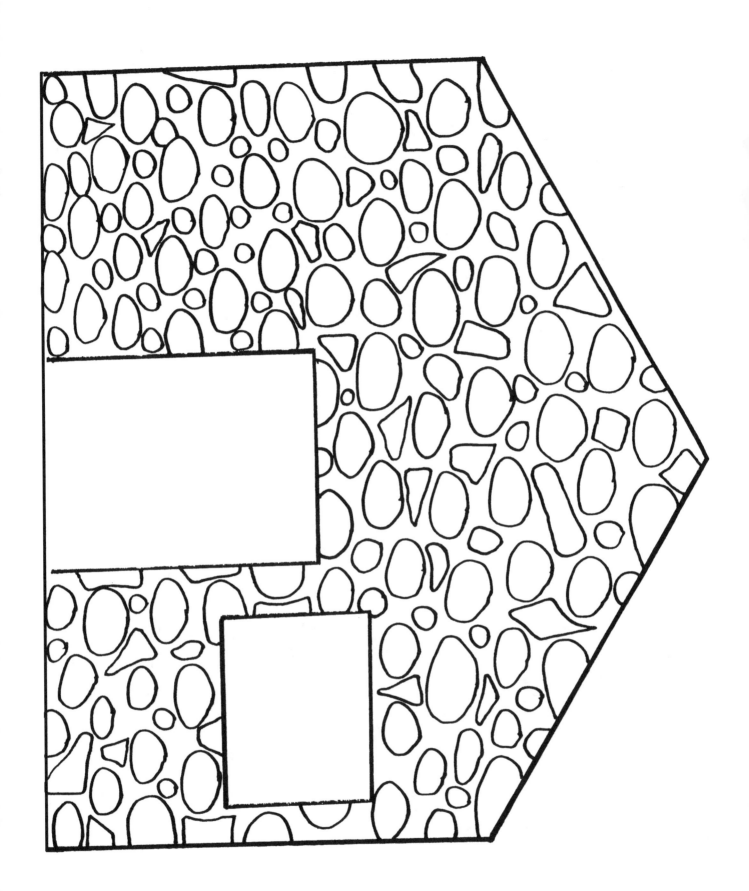

House of rocks—Enlarge on photocopier, color, and mount on cardboard.

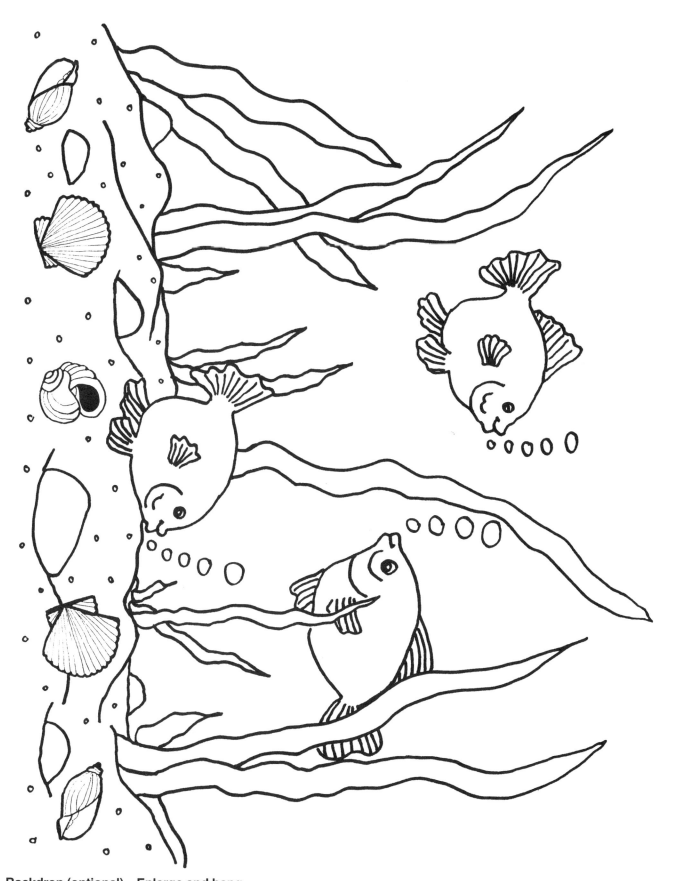

Backdrop (optional)—Enlarge and hang.

Little Red Racing Heart

A Valentine's Day Twist on "Little Red Riding Hood"

■ ■

Number of puppets: 5	**Props:**
• Red Racing Heart	• Small basket
• Pa Wolf	• Valentine (commercial)
• Ma Wolf	• Homemade Valentine (pattern, p. 30)
• Rabbit	**Setting:** Outside, small house nearby
• Turtle	**Lighting:** No special effects
Playing Time: 10–15 minutes	**Music:** Any music with fast tempo

Scene 1

Action:	*Music (approx. 20 seconds). Red Racing Heart is outside, racing about near her house, carrying basket of goodies.*
RRHeart:	Oh, I just love racing. I'm going to be a famous runner someday. I'm going to win medals and ribbons, and … *(Rabbit races on and off stage.)*
	Wow! Did you see that? There must be a race going on! I'd better see who's winning. *(Enter Turtle, slowly across stage.)*
	Oh, here's someone I can ask. *(To Turtle.)* Excuse me, Mr. Turtle, but do you know if there is a race?
Turtle:	*(Speaking slowly.)* Yes I do, and I'm in it.
RRHeart:	You're in it?
Turtle:	*(Slowly.)* Yes I am, and I'm going to win it.
RRHeart:	And how do you plan on winning it?
Turtle:	*(Slowly.)* Slow and steady wins the race. I'd love to stay and talk, Miss Heart, but I have a race to win. *(Exits.)*
RRHeart:	Hmmm. Slow and steady wins the race. That's what my mother is always saying to me! I can't believe she told me to walk all the way to Grandma's house with this basket of Valentine's gifts. I can just hear her now. *(Mimics mother's voice.)* "Now little Heart, dear, we don't want to break any of Grandma's delicious

Valentine cookies, do we? We must walk carefully to Grandma's house. We can run later." I never understood this "we" stuff. So what if a cookie or two breaks? Mother must have packed a lot of cookies. *(Peeks inside basket.)* Oh, and there's a Valentine card from us—that won't break, and some flowers—they won't break. Grandma wouldn't mind if I ran a bit. *(Begins wiggling.)* Besides, *(yelling)* I can't help myself! *(Races around stage and exits.)*

Scene 2

Action:	*Music (approx. 15 seconds). In the cave of Pa and Ma Wolf. Pa is relaxing.*
Ma Wolf:	PA! *(Pa Wolf jumps up.)*
Pa Wolf:	Yes, my love.
Ma Wolf:	Now don't ya go givin' me that "my love" stuff.
Pa Wolf:	Yes, my dear.
Ma Wolf:	Aaagh! Do ya know what today is?
Pa Wolf:	Uh, it's Wednesday. *(Substitute appropriate day of week.)*
Ma Wolf:	It's Valentine's Day, ya lugnut!
Pa Wolf:	That's nice, Dear.
Ma Wolf:	Nice! Yer supposed to give me something on Valentine's Day. Yer supposed to tell me *(raising voice)* that ya love me!
Pa Wolf:	But I do love ya, Muffin. Ya know that.
Ma Wolf:	Well that's not good enough fer today. *(Yelling.)* I want a Valentine's present. Get out of here, and don't ye come back until ye got me a present!
Pa Wolf:	Yes, My Love. *(Begins to slowly exit off stage and is run over by racing Rabbit. Pa Wolf lies still for a minute, then groans when Turtle climbs over him.)*
Turtle:	*(Walking over Wolf.)* Pardon me, Mr. Wolf, but I've got a race to win. *(Turtle exits. Wolf picks himself up and exits.)*

Scene 3

Action:	*Music (approx 15 seconds). In woods. Pa Wolf is running.*
Pa Wolf:	*(Gasping.)* I've *(puff, puff)* gotta find somethin' nice for Ma, *(puff, puff)* or she's gonna skin me. *(Runs in one direction, RRHeart runs onstage from other side and they collide in the middle.)*

RRHeart:	Oh no! Grandma's Valentine's cookies! I bet they're all smashed.
Pa Wolf:	Did you say Valentine's cookies?
RRHeart:	Yes I did. I'm taking them to Grandma for Valentine's Day.
Pa Wolf:	Why, what a sweet little Heart y' be. *(Yelling.)* Now hand over the goodies! *(Chases Heart.)*
RRHeart:	Nothin' doing, bait breath, get your own cookies. *(Smugly.)* Besides, you couldn't catch me anyway!
Pa Wolf:	Couldn't catch ya? Why, I could race circles around you, little girl. I *am* a wolf, ya know. Bet I could beat you in any race.
RRHeart:	*(Delighted.)* Ooooh, do I hear a challenge for a race? Tell you what, hairy head. I'll race you to Grandma's house—straight down this path. The first one there gets all of the cookies. On your mark, get set, GO! *(Heart races off stage.)*
Pa Wolf:	Wow! Now that's one fast young'un. Hmmm, this calls for drastic measures. I'll take the short cut to Grandma's house. *(Turns to run off stage and is run over by Rabbit. Wolf slowly gets up and races off stage in the opposite direction of Heart.)*
Turtle:	*(Entering stage, speaking slowly.)* Cookies for winning the race—now that sounds better than the race I'm in. (Turns around.) Altering course … slow and steady wins the race. *(Exits stage.)*

Scene 4

Action:	*Music (approx. 15 seconds). Outside, at edge of Grandma's house. Pa Wolf is arriving at house.*
Pa Wolf:	*(Gasping.)* Almost there *(puff, puff)*. I think I can, I think I can, I … *(Wolf is run over by Rabbit. Wolf lies on stage, groaning.)*
RRHeart:	*(Enters from opposite side of stage.)* Here I am! *(Looks at Wolf.)* Oh, oh, I'd better get inside before hairy lips gets up. *(Starts to tiptoe away.)*
Pa Wolf:	Just a minute, there, l'il Heart. I was here first.
RRHeart:	You're not at Grandma's house yet. We agreed—the first one to Grandma's house gets the cookies. *(Wolf and Heart begin arguing. As they argue, Turtle enters and walks up to Grandma's house.)*
Turtle:	*(Speaking slowly.)* Slow and steady wins the race. I told you so.
RRHeart/Pa Wolf:	*(Together, looking at Turtle.)* You mean *you* won?
Turtle:	I told you. Slow and steady wins the race. *(Takes basket and exits.)*

Pa Wolf:	Now what'm I gonna do? The Mrs. ain't gonna let me back in the house without a Valentine's present.
RRHeart:	Well, we could make some Valentines. Grandma has paper and crayons and scissors.
Pa Wolf:	Oh, and I have a fabulous red marker that I keep with me. I use it for marking short cuts in the woods.
RRHeart:	Wonderful. And maybe Grandma will let us bake some more cookies. She's a wonderful cook, you know. Come on inside, Mr. Wolf. *(Both exit.)*

Scene 5

Action:	*Music (approx. 15 seconds). In the cave of Ma and Pa Wolf. Ma is inside.*
Pa Wolf:	*(Enters cave.)* Ma! Ma, is ya home?
Ma Wolf:	Is I home? Of course I'm home.
Pa Wolf:	I brung ya a present, Ma.
Ma Wolf:	You did? You really did?
Pa Wolf:	Of course I did. Nothin's too good for my sweetheart. Here. I made ya some Valentine's cookies.
Ma Wolf:	Mmm, mmm, mmm, they smell delicious!
Pa Wolf:	Nothin' too good for my honey muffin. Here. I made you a Valentine card too. *(Bring up card.)*
Ma Wolf:	You did? Why, you's just a sweet cake. Let's see, it says: Of all other wolves you are so fine. Won't you be my Valentine? Oohhh, that's sweet!
Pa Wolf:	I would've had a nice big basket to put all of this in, but the turtle off 'n went with it.
Ma Wolf:	Turtle? What turtle?
Pa Wolf:	Never mind. Happy Valentine's Day, Ma.
Ma Wolf:	Happy Valentine's Day, Pa. *(Both exit.)*

Of all other wolves you are so fine.

Won't you be my valentine?

Wolf's valentine—Photocopy, color, cut out, and mount on stick.

The Princess and the Pumpkin

A Halloween Twist on "The Princess and the Pea"

■▪■▪■▪■▪■▪■▪■▪■▪■▪■▪■▪■▪■▪■▪■

Number of Puppets: 6	**Props:**
• King	• Telephone
• Queen	• Mattress
• Princess	
• Ghost	**Setting:** Inside castle
• Pumpkin	**Lighting:** Desk lamp to turn on and off
• Prince	**Music:** Halloween music, stormy sounds
Playing Time: 10–15 minutes	

Scene 1

Action:	*Music (approx. 20 seconds). King and Queen on stage. Sounds of thunder; a loud scream is heard.*
Queen:	Oh dear, there goes another impostor Princess.
King:	I am getting very worried dear! The time has come for our son to be married. I am getting old and tired, and I want him to take the throne. But our son must be married before he can become King.
Queen:	And how do you propose we get him married? If you remember, he *is* a pumpkin right now.
King:	Yes, yes I know. That blasted witch's spell.
Queen:	If only we could find a *real* Princess. Only a real Princess would be brave enough to break the spell. All of those phony Princesses have left here screaming at the top of their lungs.
King:	If only we could find a real Princess tonight.
Queen:	You're right! It's Halloween night. The witch said that the spell could be broken by a brave Princess …
King/Queen:	*(Together.)* On Halloween night!
Queen:	We'll have to hurry, we only have a few hours left. *(King and Queen exit.)*

Scene 2

Action: *Music (approx. 15 seconds). Storm sounds continue, Queen is using telephone, King is pacing.*

Queen: *(Talking on telephone.)* Well, yes it is the same castle you heard about, but … well no, it's not ghost-proof but … oh, for heaven's sake! It's only a little ghost! *(Hangs up phone in frustration.)*

King: *(Still pacing.)* No luck, dear?

Queen: No luck. I phoned every Princess in the local Royal Directory. There aren't a lot of Princesses in the directory, you know. I even tried a few common folk. Nobody wants to come to our castle. Everybody has heard about it. *(Begins to wail.)* Oh, it's no use. Our son is destined to be a pumpkin the rest of his life!

King: There, there, dear. Something is bound to happen. *(Loud crack of thunder.)* Wow! I have never seen such a storm in all my kingly days … or nights.

Queen: Quit your complaining and do something useful!

King: Like what, my dear?

Queen: Well *(loud knock at door)* like go and answer the door!

King: Who's there? I wonder who could be out on a night like this?

Princess: I am a Princess caught in the storm. Please let me in.

King: Oh, here we go again! Sure you are a real Princess!

Princess: But I am! Please let me in, it's raining cats and dogs!

King: *(Sympathetically.)* Come in then, out of the rain. *(To Queen.)* This girl says that she is a real Princess.

Queen: *(Examines Princess.)* Hmmmm, I've never seen you around here before.

Princess: Quite true. I come from a faraway kingdom.

King: Oh, so then you haven't heard of our castle?

Princess: *(Hesitating.)* No …

King/Queen: *(Together.)* Splendid!

Queen: You shall stay the night, then. I will make the bed in the haunted … er, in the Princess Tower. *(All exit.)*

Scene 3

Action: *Music (approx. 15 seconds). Queen and Pumpkin are on stage. Queen is making bed.*

Pumpkin: *(Whining.)* Mom, do we have to go through this again?

Queen: Of course we do. Do you want to be a pumpkin for the rest of your life?

Pumpkin: Well, no, but …

Queen: Do you want to give up the throne?

Pumpkin: Well, no, but …

Queen: Do you want to never have a wife?

Pumpkin: Hmmm, when do we start?

Queen: We start now! The Princess is on her way up the stairs. Quick! Hide under the mattress. I'll go get her.

Scene 4

Action: *Music (approx. 15 seconds). Princess arrives in room with bed.*

Princess: What a beautiful room! It was so nice of the King and Queen to let me stay here. *(Looks around.)* It's awfully dark in this room though … maybe I can light a lamp. *(Loud crash is heard.)* Who's there?

Ghost: *(Offstage.)* Just me!

Princess: Who are you?

Ghost: BOO!

Princess: You don't scare me. Now tell me, who are you?

Ghost: BOO!

Princess: Boo?

Ghost: BOO!

Princess: Boo who? *(Looks around stage.)*

Ghost: YES! *(Drifts on and offstage.)*

Princess: What? *(Looks, ghost is gone.)*

Ghost:	NO!
Princess:	*(Exasperated.)* What is your name?
Ghost:	BOO!
Princess:	Good. Now we're getting somewhere. Boo is your first name.
Ghost:	YES!
Princess:	But what is your last name?
Ghost:	HOO!
Princess:	Why you, silly. I want to know your last name.
Ghost:	It's HOO. BOO HOO.
Princess:	Boo Hoo? *(Ghost appears on stage; Princess jumps back in surprise.)* It really IS a ghost!
Ghost:	In the spirit!
Princess:	But what are you doing in a beautiful castle like this? I thought haunted houses always had smashed windows and lots and lots of cobwebs.
Ghost:	Spell.
Princess:	OK. What would you like me to spell?
Ghost:	NO! A SPELL!
Princess:	Oh I get it. You're under a spell.
Ghost:	No, the Prince is under a spell.
Princess:	The Prince? Where's the Prince?
Pumpkin:	*(Muffled sound.)* I'm under here.
Princess:	*(Looking under bed.)* You're a pumpkin!
Ghost:	YES! *(Pumpkin comes on stage.)*
Princess:	So, how do we break your spell?
Pumpkin:	Well, you have to sleep with me under your mattress all night.
Princess:	Ouch! That sounds uncomfortable!
Pumpkin:	For both of us.

Princess:	Is that it? I sleep with you under my mattress all night and the spell is broken?
Pumpkin:	*(Slowly.)* Well, that's only half the spell. You have to take BOO back to the Witch's Haunted House.
Princess:	That sounds easy enough. C'mon, let's go!
Ghost:	Who?
Princess:	Why you, Boo—who else?
Ghost:	YES! *(Princess and Ghost exit; Pumpkin rolls under bed out of sight.)*

Scene 5

Action:	*Music (approx. 15 seconds). Princess is lying fitfully on mattress, pumpkin bobs up and down under mattress. Morning sounds. Mattress goes completely flat.*
Princess:	Oh, what an awful sleep. First going to that witch's house. I think she was glad to see her ghost friend again, though. I don't think she remembered where she had left him. And then, sleeping on this mattress with a pumpkin underneath me. Who could sleep with a pumpkin underneath them? Hmmm, the mattress is pretty flat now. Gosh, I hope I didn't squash him. *(Peeks under mattress.)* Oh Mr. Pumpkin, are you there? *(Muffled voice responds.)* I say, Mr. Pumpkin, are you there?
Prince:	*(Muffled.)* I'm under here! *(Mattress begins to lift and Prince emerges with pumpkin stem on head.)* Oh boy, I'm back to me!
Princess:	*(Looking at stem.)* Almost.
Prince:	Oh never mind that! Let's go tell my parents that the spell has been lifted! *(Both exit stage.)*

Scene 6

Action:	*Music (approx. 15 seconds). Queen is onstage with Ghost, arguing. Enter Prince and Princess.*
Ghost:	BOO!
Queen:	Oh, for heaven's sake! Stop that nonsense!
Prince:	Look Mother, it's me! The spell has been broken!
Queen:	Never mind that now! Help me get rid of this pesky ghost! I sent your father for some traps.

Princess:	Boo, why are you back here? I took you home last night.
Ghost:	It's more fun here.
Prince:	But Boo, I'm not a pumpkin anymore. I'm a Prince. Who will keep you company?
Ghost:	*(Floating around room to each person.)* You … and you … and you … that's who!
Queen:	Hmmm. Well, Ghost, do you like parties!
Ghost:	YES!
Queen:	Well, that's good, because there's going to be a really big party here. The Prince and Princess are going to be married.
Ghost:	YES! And I can decorate the hall, and welcome the guests … and I can catch the BOO-quet!

Music (approx. 15 seconds).

Little Green O'Glenn and the Lazy Leprechauns

A St. Patrick's Day Twist on "The Little Red Hen"

Number of Puppets: 4
- Leprechaun 1
- Leprechaun 2
- Leprechaun 3
- Little Green O'Glenn (a green hen)

Playing Time: 10–15 minutes

Props:
- Small broom
- Small watering can
- Bundle of wheat
- Bag of flour
- Bread
- Gold coins
- Table

Setting: Outside Little Green O'Glenn's house

Lighting: No special effects

Music: Irish music, jigs or reels

Scene 1

Action: *Music (approx. 20 seconds). O'Glenn is outside her house with broom.*

O'Glenn: Just look at the mess here. I only swept this walk last week. I guess I'll have to do it again.

Leprechaun 1: *(Approaching.)* Top 'o the morn to you, Miss O'Glenn.

O'Glenn: Good day, Sir.

Leprechaun 1: It's a lovely establishment you have here, me lass.

O'Glenn: Thank you.

Leprechaun 1: You know, I've been searchin' the country for a place such as this.

O'Glenn: You have? For what?

Leprechaun 1: Why for to rest me weary bones, that is.

O'Glenn: I'm sorry, Sir. I think you have misunderstood. You see, I'm not …

Leprechaun 1: Yes indeed, it will be just the spot for some rest and relaxation.

O'Glenn: But this isn't …

Leprechaun 1:	Now don't you trouble yourself, lass. I'll make meself at home. *(Exits stage behind house.)*
O'Glenn:	Oh dear. Now how am I going to explain to him that he can't stay here.
Leprechaun 2:	*(Approaching.)* Top 'o the morn to you, Miss O'Glenn.
O'Glenn:	Good day to you, sir.
Leprechaun 2:	I'm looking for me friend—looks a little like me, he does.
O'Glenn:	Yes, I saw him. He went inside my house.
Leprechaun 2:	Hmmm. Lovely establishment you have here.
O'Glenn:	That's what your friend said. Now about your friend … could you tell him that he must leave my …
Leprechaun 2:	Aye, I would be more than happy to go inside and retrieve me friend.
O'Glenn:	No, you wait here. I'll go get him.
Leprechaun 2:	Wouldn't be hearing of bothering you in that way, me lass. I'll be going inside meself.
O'Glenn:	But …
Leprechaun 2:	Tut, tut, don't you be bothering yerself. I'll be getting me friend. *(Exits stage behind house.)*
O'Glenn:	Oh dear. I bet the two of them will stay in there. Now what will I do?
Leprechaun 3:	*(Approaching.)* Top 'o the morn to you, Miss O'Glenn.
O'Glenn:	Good day to you, sir. I hope you're here to get your two friends.
Leprechaun 3:	Then you've seen them, you have.
O'Glenn:	Oh, I've seen them alright. They went right inside my house.
Leprechaun 3:	And a lovely establishment it would be.
O'Glenn:	That's what your friends said.
Leprechaun 3:	Now, if you will but bid me pass, I'll be goin' inside to get me two friends. *(Starts inside.)*
O'Glenn:	*(Jumps in front of doorway.)* Oh no you don't! Two uninvited guests in my home is enough. You're not getting in too!
Leprechaun 3:	If you be sayin' so, me lass. *(Looks up in sky.)* Well! Would you be lookin' at that?

O'Glenn:	*(Looks up.)* Looking at what?
Leprechaun 3:	Why at the rainbow, of course. Brightest one me eyes have ever seen.
O'Glenn:	*(Looking.)* I don't see it!
Leprechaun 3:	Right over there, me love. *(Points away from house.)*
O'Glenn:	*(Turns away from house.)* I still don't see it.
Leprechaun 3:	*(Sneaks into house, exits stage.)* Hee, hee, hee, can't stop me!
O'Glenn:	Oh dear. I came outside to sweep my sidewalk, and now I have three leprechauns in my house. *(Sweeps, then exits stage.)*

Scene 2

Action:	*Music (approx. 15 seconds). Inside O'Glenn's house.*
Leprechaun 2:	Now me dear Miss O'Glenn, we need to be talking about the menus of this establishment. We've been dining on nothing but bird seed for the past few days.
O'Glenn:	Well, Mr. Leprechaun. That would be because I'm a bird. Birds do eat bird seed, you know. If you would like something different to eat, I suggest you go out and find it.
Leprechaun 3:	Now me dear, perhaps you might buy us a wee bit of food at the market. I'm sure it would be no trouble to you at all.
O'Glenn:	I suppose I could do that. As soon as you pay me for the room and board, I'll go down to the market.
Leprechaun 1:	Oh, I just heard me friend outside. *(Exits quickly.)*
Leprechaun 3:	Would you look at that, another rainbow. *(Exits quickly.)*
Leprechaun 2:	Now where do you suppose they went? I'll be goin' after them. *(Exits quickly.)*
O'Glenn:	It's the same every time! Every time I mention money, they all run away. Maybe I should just forget about the whole thing. I think I'll go for a walk. *(Exits.)*

Scene 3

Action:	*Music (approx. 15 seconds). Leprechauns are inside house, lazing about.*
O'Glenn:	*(Enters.)* Quick! Come see what I found! *(Leprechauns gather around.)*

Leprechaun 1:	Is it a piece of gold?
Leprechaun 3:	Better yet would be a pot of gold!
O'Glenn:	I have a grain of wheat!
Leprechauns:	*(Together, disappointed.)* Wheat?
Leprechaun 2:	What would ye be wantin' to do with a wee bit of wheat?
O'Glenn:	Don't you see? We can plant this grain and grow some wheat.
Leprechaun 1:	Aye, I suppose it would be a worthwhile venture.
O'Glenn:	Then it's agreed! So, who will help me plant the grain? *(Leprechauns fall over each other trying to get outside.)*
Leprechaun 2:	Off for a wee bit of fresh air, I am. *(Exits quickly.)*
Leprechaun 3:	I cannot believe me eyes. There's that rainbow again! *(Exits quickly.)*
Leprechaun 1:	I'll just go with them. *(Exits quickly.)*
O'Glenn:	Well, I guess I'll have to plant the wheat myself. *(Exits.)*

Scene 4

Action:	*Music (approx. 15 seconds). Leprechauns are inside house, lazing about.*
O'Glenn:	*(Enters with watering can.)* Hello sirs, would you mind …
Leprechaun 2:	Why the sweet little thing—she's bringing us some refreshments.
Leprechaun 3:	Mind that the drink is good and cold, me love.
O'Glenn:	This water's not for you. It's for the wheat.
Leprechaun 1:	Oh. Well I suppose the plant might be wanting a sip or two as well.
O'Glenn:	Then it's agreed! So, who will help me water the wheat? *(Leprechauns fall over each other trying to get outside.)*
Leprechaun 1:	Me toes are in need of a walk, they be. *(Exits quickly.)*
Leprechaun 3:	Never saw a rainbow come and go as this one does. *(Exits quickly.)*
Leprechaun 2:	Now don't ye be worrying, Miss O'Glenn. I'll go fetch the two of them and have them back here in no time. *(Exits quickly.)*
O'Glenn:	Looks like it's up to me again. I'll have to water the wheat myself. *(Exits with watering can.)*

Scene 5

Action:	*Music (approx. 15 seconds). Leprechauns are inside dancing a jig to Irish music.*
O'Glenn:	*(Enters.)* Mr. Leprechauns, I have some good news!
Leprechaun 2:	And what would that be, me dear?
Leprechaun 1:	Did ye find a pot of gold?
Leprechaun 3:	At the end of me rainbow?
O'Glenn:	No, of course not. But I did cut down my wheat, and I have a big bag of it to take to the mill to be ground.
Leprechauns:	*(Together, disinterested.)* Ooohhh.
O'Glenn:	So, who will help me take the wheat to the mill? *(Leprechauns fall over each other trying to get outside.)*
Leprechaun 2:	Would ye look at that? Me toes are still tappin' to the music. Can't seem to stop them, I say. *(Exits quickly.)*
Leprechaun 3:	Why, he'd be tappin' his way straight to the rainbow. *(Exits quickly.)*
Leprechaun 1:	I'd better be goin' after the lot. They might get lost, you know. *(Exits quickly.)*
O'Glenn:	*(Sighs heavily.)* Very well, I'll take the wheat to the mill myself. *(Exits.)*

Scene 6

Action:	*Music (approx. 15 seconds). O'Glenn is inside baking bread. Gold coins are on table.*
O'Glenn:	*(Brings bread to table.)* Mmmm. That smells so good.
Leprechaun 2:	*(Enters.)* What would be that lovely smell I be smelling?
Leprechaun 1:	*(Enters.)* Mmm. I hope that would be our supper I be sniffin'.
Leprechaun 3:	*(Enters, sniffing.)* What a wonderful smell that would be.
O'Glenn:	It's bread I made from some of the flour I took to the mill. I sold most of it, but I kept enough to make a loaf of fresh bread.
Leprechaun 1:	You sold the wheat, you say.
Leprechaun 2:	Why that would mean you'd be bringing home some … *(Leprechauns look at table.)*
Leprechauns:	*(Together.)* GOLD!

Leprechaun 1:	Glory be to the shamrocks! Gold it is!
Leprechaun 3:	Now me dear Miss O'Glenn. Why don't we be sitting down around the table and samplin' yer fine bread. And while we're doin' that, we'll be dividin' the gold coins ye have.
O'Glenn:	Ho! Ho! So now you want to share! You want to help me eat the bread. But you wouldn't help me plant the wheat. Nobody helped me water it, or mill, or make the bread.
Leprechaun 2:	*(Pleading.)* We were so weak from hunger, me dear!
O'Glenn:	*(Angry.)* Weak from hunger? You were dancing a jig! You're nothing but a bunch of lazy, short people, and I've put up with you as long as I can. Get out before I peck your eyes out. Where's my broom? *(Chases Leprechauns out, making clucking noises.)*
Leprechauns:	*(Run from house, yelling.)*
O'Glenn:	Alone at last! Now I can really enjoy the fruits of my labor. Mmmm, it was worth all the work. This is the best bread I've ever tasted!

Music (approx. 15 seconds).

The Three Easter Bunnies Gruff

An Easter Twist on "The Three Billy Goats Gruff"

■ ▪ ■ ▪ ■ ▪ ■ ▪ ■ ▪ ■ ▪ ■ ▪ ■ ▪ ■ ▪ ■ ▪ ■ ▪ ■ ▪ ■ ▪ ■ ▪ ■ ▪ ■ ▪ ■

Number of puppets: 4
- Big Easter Bunny
- Middle Easter Bunny
- Little Easter Bunny
- Candy Troll

Playing Time: 10–15 minutes

Props:
- Bridge
- Chimney

- Four Easter baskets (small, medium, large, extra large with candy)
- Two signs (Santa Welcome; Santa and Easter Bunnies Gruff Welcome—see patterns on pgs. 45–46)

Setting: Two meadows connected by a bridge at center stage

Lighting: No special effects

Music: Light spring or Easter music

Scene 1

Action:	*Music (approx. 20 seconds). Easter Bunnies arrive on stage one by one. All are on same side of bridge.*
Little Bunny:	*(Pretending to hide eggs from basket.)* Here we go, hippety hop, an egg I drop … hide one here, hide one there.
Middle Bunny:	We're all done hiding Easter eggs in this meadow, brothers. What are we going to do now?
Little Bunny:	*(Pointing to other side of bridge.)* We could go over there.
Big Bunny:	I'm afraid not, brothers. We have to be satisfied hiding our eggs on this side of the bridge. You know what Grandfather Gruff told us about the Candy Troll. Remember when he stopped Grandfather on the bridge and ate all of his Easter eggs? We almost didn't give Easter baskets that year.
Middle Bunny:	Ooooh, that makes me hopping mad to think that the children on the other side of the bridge won't have a candy-filled Easter because of that Candy Troll.
Little Bunny:	*(Sniffing.)* Those poor boys and girls.

Middle Bunny:	*(Looking at big brother.)* We should at least try.
Big Bunny:	*(Hesitating.)* Well, maybe you're right. Maybe we can come up with a plan to cross the bridge.
Middle Bunny:	And I have JUST THE PLAN!
Big Bunny/Little Bunny:	*(Together.)* We're all ears brother! *(Bunnies huddle together and whisper.)*

Scene 2

Action:	*Music (approx. 15 seconds). Little Bunny is preparing to cross bridge; Candy Troll is hiding under bridge.*
Little Bunny:	Hippety hop, hippety hop, I'm crossing the bridge and I won't stop. Hippety hop, hippety hop, I'm crossing the bridge and I won't …
Candy Troll:	STOP! *(Jumps to middle of bridge.)*
Little Bunny:	*(To audience.)* Oh nnnno, it's the Cccandy Tttroll!
Candy Troll:	*(Harshly.)* Who's that on my roof? *(Then gently.)* Is that you, Santa?
Little Bunny:	Nnnoo, sssir, it's the Little Easter Bunny Gruff. I jjjust wwwanted to cross the bridge to get to the other meadow so I could …
Candy Troll:	*(Angrily.)* This is not a bridge. It's the roof to my house, and only Santa is allowed on my roof. He'll land on my roof, and come down my chimney and bring me … *(pausing)* … wait a minute, who did you say you were?
Little Bunny:	I'm the Little Easter Bunny Gruff. I just want to cross the bridge … er, your roof, to get to the other meadow.
Candy Troll:	Hmmm … Easter Bunny you say … and Easter Bunnies bring CANDY!! *(Candy Troll jumps closer to Little Bunny and inspects basket of candy, small chase ensues.)*
Little Bunny:	Eeeek! No, ppplease don't hurt me! I'm just a small scrawny bbbbunny!
Candy Troll:	You're sure right about that. Who'd want to eat you. I just want your CANDY! *(Jumps up and down.)*
Little Bunny:	*(Becoming braver.)* This little bit of candy? Why I have the smallest Easter basket of all the Easter Bunnies. If you let me cross the bridge … er, your roof, my brother will follow, and he has a much bigger basket of candy than me.
Candy Troll:	*(Annoyed.)* Oh, all right. I'll wait for him to step on my roof. You'd better hurry across before I change my mind. *(Crawls back under bridge.)*

Little Bunny:	Hippety hop, hippety hop, I'm crossing the bridge and I won't stop. Hippety hop, hippety hop, I'm crossing the bridge and I won't stop … (*Crosses to other side and exits.*)

Scene 3

Action:	*Music (approx. 15 seconds). Middle Bunny is preparing to cross bridge; Candy Troll is hiding under bridge.*
Middle Bunny:	Hippety hop, hippety hop, I'm crossing the bridge,and I won't stop. Hippety hop, hippety hop, I'm crossing the bridge and I won't …
Candy Troll:	STOP! (*Jumps to middle of bridge.*)
Middle Bunny:	(*To audience.*) Oh bbbooy, it's the Cccandy Tttroll, and he's rreally bbbig!
Candy Troll:	(*Harshly.*) Who's that on my roof? (*Then gently.*) Is that you, Santa?
Middle Bunny:	Nnnot rreally. I'm actually the Middle Easter Bunny Gruff. I wanted to cross the bridge to get to the other meadow so I could …
Candy Troll:	(*Angrily.*) This is not a bridge. It's the roof to my house, and only Santa is allowed on my roof. He'll land on my roof, and come down my chimney and bring me … (*pausing*) … wait a minute, who did you say you were?
Middle Bunny:	I'm the Middle Easter Bunny Gruff. I was just looking for my brother. I think he went this way. I saw him crossing the bridge … er … your roof.
Candy Troll:	Hmmm, Middle Easter Bunny Gruff. Yes, yes, now I remember. Yes, your brother did walk on my roof. He told me that you were coming, and that you had a big basket of CANDY! (*Candy Troll jumps closer to Middle Bunny and inspects basket of candy, small chase ensues.*)
Middle Bunny:	Ooooh! Please, please don't eat me. I'm not really that bbbig of a bbbunny.
Candy Troll:	Where do all you rabbits get the idea I want to eat you? Maybe a story you read somewhere? I told your brother, and now I'm telling you. I don't want to eat you. I just want your CANDY! (*Jumps up and down.*)
Middle Bunny:	(*Becoming braver.*) That's all you want? My candy? Gee, I thought a big, strong troll like you would want a bigger basket than mine.
Candy Troll:	Bigger? Do you mean there's a bigger basket than yours?
Middle Bunny:	Of course there is. My brother, the Big Easter Bunny Gruff has the biggest Easter basket of all … filled right to the rim.
Candy Troll:	With candy?

Middle Bunny:	Why, of course with candy. Every kind you can imagine. Now, you could take my candy, or you could let me cross the bridge … er, your roof, and take my brother's basket. He should be right behind me.
Candy Troll:	*(Annoyed.)* Oh, all right. I'll wait for your big brother to set foot on my roof. Hurry along then, before I change my mind. *(Crawls back under bridge.)*
Middle Bunny:	Hippety hop, hippety hop, I'm crossing the bridge and I won't stop. Hippety hop, hippety hop, I'm crossing the bridge and I won't stop … *(Crosses to other side and exits.)*

Scene 4

Action:	*Music (approx. 15 seconds). Big Bunny is preparing to cross bridge; Candy Troll is hiding under bridge.*
Big Bunny:	Hippety hop, hippety hop, I'm crossing the bridge and I won't stop. Hippety hop, hippety hop, I'm crossing the bridge and I won't …
Candy Troll:	STOP! *(Jumps to middle of bridge.)*
Big Bunny:	*(To audience.)* Yep, that's the Candy Troll all right … just how Grandfather Gruff described him.
Candy Troll:	*(Harshly.)* Who's that on my roof? *(Then gently.)* Is that you, Santa?
Big Bunny:	Santa? Why would Santa cross this bridge?
Candy Troll:	*(Angrily.)* This is not a bridge! How many times do I have to tell you dumb bunnies? This is the roof to my house, and only Santa is allowed on my roof. He'll land on my roof, and come down my chimney, and bring me all kinds of presents and … CANDY!
Big Bunny:	Chimney? You don't have a chimney!
Candy Troll:	I don't?
Big Bunny:	No, you don't. How is Santa going to come down your chimney if you don't have one?
Candy Troll:	*(Sniffing.)* I … I don't know. Maybe that's why he's never come before. I thought it was all those stories he'd heard about me eating other animals. It's not true, you know. *(Sobbing.)* I just wanted some candy.
Big Bunny:	There, there, don't cry. *(Candy Troll wails.)* I'll tell you what—why don't we build you a chimney. I know there are plenty of rocks in the meadow I just came from. Why don't we gather up some rocks and make a chimney?

Candy Troll:	*(Sniffing.)* You'd do that for me?
Big Bunny:	Of course I would. We Easter Bunnies are pretty generous creatures, you know. We've been known to give things to people. *(Looks for rocks.)* There! There's some nice rocks for a chimney.
Candy Troll:	*(Pausing.)* Have Easter Bunnies ever given anything to, say Candy Trolls? Santa gives to everybody. *(Works on chimney.)* I'm sure Santa will like this chimney.
Big Bunny:	*(Working on chimney.)* Hmmm. Candy to Candy Trolls … I'll have to talk to my brothers about that. There! Your chimney is done. Let's put it into place. *(Place chimney behind bridge.)*
Candy Troll:	Oooh, thank you! *(Pausing.)* You know, you Easter Bunnies aren't so bad after all. You may use my roof to cross to the other meadow.
Big Bunny:	Thanks, Mr. Troll. The boys and girls of the meadow will get lots of candy this year. Hippety hop, hippety hop, I'm crossing the bridge and I won't stop. Hippety hop, hippety hop, I'm crossing the bridge and I won't stop. *(Crosses to other side and exits.)*
Candy Troll:	ROOF! *(To audience.)* How many times do I have to tell those dumb bunnies! *(Crawls back under bridge.)*

Scene 5

Action:	*Music (approx. 15 seconds). Three Easter Bunnies Gruff are together in the new meadow.*
Little Bunny:	*(Bouncing up and down.)* Yippee! Now we get to hide Easter eggs in this meadow. Won't the boys and girls be happy? *(Pretending to hide eggs.)* Hippety hop, an egg I drop …
Middle Bunny:	Hide one here, hide one there … *(Pretending to hide eggs.)* The children will be so surprised!
Big Bunny:	You know, we never would have been able to do this if it weren't for the Candy Troll.
Middle Bunny:	He did let us pass.
Little Bunny:	I wonder if he'll let us pass next year.
Big Bunny:	I'm sure he would if we left him a little something this year.
Middle Bunny:	Maybe we should leave him something every year. He's not really so bad.

Big Bunny: It's agreed then! The Candy Troll is on our list. *(All together shout Hooray!)*

(Bunnies leave enormous basket of candy at base of bridge and exit stage.)

Scene 6

Action: *Music (approx. 15 seconds). Candy Troll is under bridge. He begins to wake up.*

Candy Troll: *(Yawning.)* So, today is the day the Big Easter Bunny Gruff was telling me about. Easter. Hmmm, I wonder if the children in the meadow are finding their presents. I'll go outside and watch. *(Starts out from under bridge.)*

What's this? Oh, my goodness, it's a GREAT BIG BASKET OF … CANDY!! There's a tag on it too. It says "to the Candy Troll from the Easter Bunnies." YIPPEE! YIPPEE! Time to celebrate! But WAIT! I have one thing to do first … *(Tears down "Santa Welcome" sign and puts up new "Santa and Easter Bunnies Gruff Welcome" sign.)*

Music (approx. 15 seconds).

Sign—Photocopy, color, cut out, and mount on stick.

Santa Welcome!

and Easter Bunnies Gruff

Sign—Photocopy, color, cut out, and mount on stick.

Zip Van Blinkle

A Time Travel Twist on "Rip Van Winkle"

■▪■▪■▪■▪■▪■▪■▪■▪■▪■▪■▪■▪■▪■▪■▪■

Number of Puppets: 9	**Playing Time:** 15 minutes
• Zip	**Props:**
• Wife	• Time machine
• Caveman (looks like Zip)	
• Cavewoman (looks like Wife)	**Setting:** Outside, small house nearby
• 50's Man (looks like Zip)	
• 50's Woman (looks like Wife)	**Lighting:** No special effects
• Future Man (looks like Zip)	
• Future Woman (looks like Wife)	**Music:** Specific to each scene—longer time
• Troll	than other puppet shows

Note: The Man and Woman pairs all look alike, but they are dressed differently.

Scene 1

Action:	*Music (suggestion: "Zip a Dee Do Da," approx. 30 seconds). Enter Zip, casually strolling.*
Wife:	ZIP! *(Zip starts running and wife chases, they enter from opposite sides and run into each other.)*
Zip:	Oh, hello Dear.
Wife:	Don't you "hello Dear" me, Mr. Van Blinkle. Where have you been all day?
Zip:	Well, I …
Wife:	Never mind where you've been all day. Why haven't you been home to fix the well?
Zip:	Well, I …
Wife:	Never mind why you haven't been home. Well, go get me some water from the stream.
Zip:	But there's a hole in the bucket, Dear Sweet Pea …
Wife:	AAAgh! Don't start that routine with me again. Now go get the water NOW!

Zip:	Yes, Sweet Pea.
Wife:	And don't "Sweet Pea" me!
Zip:	Yes, Dear. *(Exits singing "There's a hole in the bucket." Wife exits, too.)*

Scene 2

Action:	*Music (approx. 15 seconds). Enter Zip, strolling.*
Zip:	There's a hole in the bucket …
Troll:	*(Offstage.)* Then fix it, Van Blinkle …
Zip:	Who's there! Is that you, Sweet Pea?
Troll:	*(Enters.)* Sweet Pea, Sweet Pea, hee hee hee hee hee.
Zip:	What do you want?
Troll:	What do I want? No, no, no. What do I have!
Zip:	What do you have?
Troll:	Funny you should ask. I have a time machine. *(Bring time machine on stage.)*
Zip:	A time machine?
Troll:	A time machine! Here, try it out!
Zip:	*(Hesitating.)* What do I do with it?
Troll:	What do you do with it?
Zip:	*(Amused.)* I asked you first.
Troll:	You travel in time.
Zip:	You travel in time?
Troll:	You travel in time!
Zip:	Why would you want to do that?
Troll:	Why would you want to do that?
Zip:	*(Amused.)* I asked you first!
Troll:	Haven't you ever wanted to just get away?

Zip:	Well, I …
Troll:	Haven't you ever wanted to see what it's like in other times and places?
Zip:	Well, I …
Troll:	Haven't you ever wondered why buttered bread always falls face down on the floor?
Zip:	Well, I … what?
Troll:	Never mind, just something I always wanted to know. You just get in the machine, set the time, push the red button, and presto!
Zip:	*(Repeating.)* I just get in, set the time, push the red button, and presto! Is that it? *(Turns, Troll is gone. Enters time machine.)* I just get in *(yawns)*, set the time, push the red button, and … *(Starts to sleep. Time machine makes noises.)*

■▪■▪■▪■▪■▪■▪■▪■▪■▪■▪■▪■▪■▪■

Scene 3

Action:	*Time machine noises; Zip wakes up inside machine.*
Zip:	Oh, oh, I think I overslept. Sweet Pea's going to be mad. I wonder where I am? *(Chuckles.)* No, I wonder WHEN I am. *(Music—prehistoric, i.e., Flintstones theme, approx. 30 seconds. Zip peeks outside. Dinosaur roars and Zip screams—peeks out again and sees Caveman.)*
Zip:	*(To Caveman.)* Excuse me, but have you seen … *(Caveman runs by, Cavewoman follows, yelling with club in hand, making primitive sounds. Chase ensues throughout music.)* Funny, she looks familiar somehow. Gee, I don't think this is the time for me. I'll try again. *(Steps inside machine.)* Just a little bit forward. Now, I set the time *(yawns)*, push the red button, and … *(Falls asleep. Time machine makes noises.)*

■▪■▪■▪■▪■▪■▪■▪■▪■▪■▪■▪■▪■

Scene 4

Action:	*Time machine noises; Zip wakes up inside machine.*
Zip:	Oh, oh, overslept again. I wonder what I'll see now? *(Music—50's style, i.e.: "At the Hop," approx. 30 seconds. 50's Man running, 50's Woman chasing him.)*
Zip:	Excuse me, but … *(50's Man runs offstage, then onstage on the other side; 50's Woman chases.)*
50's Man:	Oh, you gotta help me, man, she's catching up!
Zip:	Well, I …

50's Woman:	*(Entering.)* Chip! Chip Van Stinkle! You promised to pin me tonight! You're not getting out of it this time! Chip! *(Chase ensues as music plays.)*
Zip:	Funny, she reminds me of someone, but I can't think of who. I don't think this is the time where I belong either. I'll just step back inside. *(Steps inside machine.)* Now, I just set the time *(yawns)*, push the red button, and … *(Sleeps. Time machine makes noises.)*

■▪■▪■▪■▪■▪■▪■▪■▪■▪■▪■▪■▪■▪■▪■▪■▪■▪■▪

Scene 5

Action:	*Time machine noises; Zip wakes up inside machine.*
Zip:	Oh, my goodness, I overslept again. I wonder when I am now. *(Peeks outside and Future Man goes by.)* Excuse me, but could you tell me … *(Music—futuristic, approx. 30 seconds. Future Man runs by, Future Woman runs after, making bleeping sounds. Long chase as Zip tries to communicate.)*
Zip:	Now I could swear I've seen her somewhere before. My, oh my, this time travel is exhausting. Maybe I'll just crawl back inside and travel back a bit. *(Goes inside time machine.)* Maybe I'll get back home. Now, let's see, I just get in *(yawns)*, set the time, push the red button, and … *(Starts to sleep. Time machine makes noises.)*

■▪■▪■▪■▪■▪■▪■▪■▪■▪■▪■▪■▪■▪■▪■▪■▪■▪■▪

Scene 6

Action:	*Time machine noises; Zip wakes up inside machine.*
Zip:	Hmmm, I think this is pretty close to home. I'd better check it out quietly. Very quietly. *(Peeks out and Wife is right there. Music, approx. 30 seconds. Chase ensues.)*
Wife:	Zip! Zip Van Blinkle!
Zip:	Hello, Sweet Pea.
Wife:	Don't you "Sweet Pea" me!
Zip:	Yes, Dear.
Wife:	Three days! You've been gone three days! Where have you been for three days!
Zip:	You wouldn't believe what …
Wife:	Now don't start making any silly excuses. You've been up to no good!
Zip:	But I …
Wife:	Don't try to get out of this one, Mr. Van Blinkle. *(Pauses, looks at time machine.)* What is this thing, anyway?

Zip: A time machine, Dear.

Wife: A time machine? Don't be foolish, Zip. It's not a time machine.

Zip: But really, it …

Wife: Now don't you try to pull anything over on me! I'll just see for myself what you're hiding in there. *(Steps inside.)* What are all these buttons?

Zip: Time dials, Dear.

Wife: Time dials, indeed! I'm turning them and nothing's even happening.

Zip: I wouldn't do that, Dear.

Wife: Don't tell me what to do, Mr. Van Blinkle. I'll figure this contraption out on my own. *(Muttering.)* I wonder what this red button is for.

Zip: *(Alarmed.)* Don't touch the red button, Sweet Pea!

Wife: I'll touch it if I want! There! *(Machine makes noises, dinosaur roars, wife screams and gradually fades offstage.)*

Zip: *(Stands at door of machine.)* Sweet Pea? Are you there? *(Looks to audience.)* Oops!

Music (suggestion: "Zip a Dee Do Da," approx. 20 seconds).

Triceralocks and the Saber-tooth Bears

A Prehistoric Twist on "Goldilocks and the Three Bears"

■ ■ ■ ■ ■ ■ ■ ■ ■ ■ ■ ■ ■   ■ ■ ■ ■

Number of Puppets: 5

- Triceralocks
- Ma Saber-tooth Bear
- Pa Saber-tooth Bear
- Baby Saber-tooth Bear
- Octopus

Playing Time: 15 minutes

Props:

- Table with three bowls
- Reptile (pattern, p. 54)

- Rocks to make rock chair
- Small feather pillows to make feather chair
- Large bed with sticks
- Medium bed with brown coating
- Small bed

Setting: Cave

Lighting: No special effects

Music: Dinosaur music

Scene 1

Action:	*Music (approx. 20 seconds). At home of bears. Table with three bowls is onstage.*
Pa:	MMMM, MMMM! Them fern flakes sure smell good, Ma. Dish me up some of them grits.
Ma:	Land sakes, it's hot, Pa. *(Dialogue between Ma and Pa. Baby tries to speak, but keeps being interrupted.)*
Baby:	EXCUSE ME!
Ma/Pa:	*(Together.)* WHAT?
Baby:	My fern flakes are hot, too.
Pa:	Alright boy, we'll go out for a walk in the woods. That'll build us some swell appetite.
Ma:	Fine idea, Pa. It'll do us good to stretch our legs. *(Dialogue between Ma and Pa. Baby tries to speak but keeps being interrupted.)*
Baby:	EXCUSE ME!

Ma/Pa:	*(Together.)* WHAT?
Baby:	BUT I DON'T WANNA GO!
Pa:	Ah, enough of that, boy. Why don't you go out and look for a nice present for your Ma. Maybe some flowers or somethin'. *(Bears exit as music begins.)*

Scene 2

Action:	*Music continues (approx. 15 seconds). Triceralocks arrives in cave.*
Triceralocks:	Oh, I wonder where I am. I've been out walking for hours, and I haven't seen anybody. Wait, what's this? A cave. My, what an interesting place. Imagine! A cave way out here in the middle of nowhere. It's pretty nice too. Hello! Is anyone home? Gosh, I wonder who lives here. Here's a table and—oh look! Three bowls of fern flakes! I just love fern flakes, and I'm so hungry after walking so long. *(Tries first bowl.)* Oh, this one is too hot. I might burn my mouth on this one. I'll try the next one. *(Tries next bowl.)* Oh, this one is too cold. Fern flakes are just no good if they're too cold. I'll try the last bowl. *(Tries baby bowl.)* Mmmm! This is just right. *(Eats from bowl.)*
	Well, those fern flakes just hit the spot. But I'm sure getting tired now after all that walking. I think my feet need a rest. Oh, I see a chair over there. I'll just pull it up here and have a relaxing rest. *(Bring rock chair up on stage—pretend to sit.)* Ouch! This chair is much too hard for me. I'll just put it back where I found it. Oh, here's another chair, I'll pull it up here and see how it is. *(Bring up feather chair—pretend to sit.)* Aa-aaa-aaaaa-CHOO! Oh, dear *(sneeze).* This chair must have Archeopterix feathers in it *(sneeze)* and I'm soooo allergic to them. AAAAACHOOOOO! *(Blows nose.)* I'll have to put this chair back, too. Oh, another chair. I'll just pull this one up and see how it is. *(Octopus puppet pulled onstage, upside down as a chair. Triceralocks sits on puppet.)* Now this is a lovely chair, very comfortable and very roomy. It must be some kind of plant, because it's very soft and cushy.
	(Music—Triceralocks pretends to be comfortable in chair as it begins to move—struggle ensues.)
Triceralocks:	I, I, I ttthink I'm a little shaky after that. Maybe I should lie down for a little while. I think I'll just go see if there are any beds. There were three bowls of fern flakes and three chairs, so I'm guessing there will be three beds. *(Arrives upstairs.)* Just as I guessed—three beds. I'll try this one first. *(Brings bed onto stage.)* Oh, it's too prickly. I think it might have some sticks or thorns in it. No, I'll put this one back and try the next one. *(Brings next bed onto stage—make slopping sounds.)* Now this one must have mud in it. It's sooo sticky. No, this will never do. I'll just bring out the last bed and ... *(Brings bed out and drops into it.)* Oh! It's perfect! I think I'll just pull this bed off to the side and take a little nap.

Scene 3

Action:	*Music (approx. 15 seconds). Triceralocks is slowly moved offstage; Saber-tooth Bears enter.*
Ma:	Well, that was refreshing, weren't it Pa?
Baby:	Excuse me ... *(Tries to speak, but is interrupted.)*
Pa:	Mmmm, yes it was honey bear. I'm sure ready for those fern flakes now.
Baby:	Excuse me ... *(Tries to speak, but is interrupted.)*
Ma:	I'll just pull up the chairs for us all.
Baby:	*(Loudly.)* EXCUSE ME!
Ma/Pa:	*(Together.)* WHAT?
Baby:	I brought you a present. *(Shows Reptile.)*
Ma:	EEEK! Land sakes, child, get that reptile out of my house! Then sit down at this table and have your breakfast.
Pa:	Somebody has been eating my fern flakes!
Baby:	Excuse me ... *(Tries to speak but is interrupted.)*
Ma:	Somebody has been eating my fern flakes! *(Ma and Pa discuss fern flakes while Baby tries to speak.)*
Baby:	*(Loudly.)* EXCUSE ME!
Ma/Pa:	*(Together.)* WHAT?
Baby:	Somebody has been eating my fern flakes and ate them all up!
Pa:	I reckon this needs a little investigatin'. Let's go into the living room. *(All go offstage. Baby comes back with chair.)*
Pa:	Somebody has been sitting in my chair!
Baby:	Excuse me ... *(Tries to speak but is interrupted.)*
Ma:	Somebody has been sitting in my chair! *(Ma and Pa discuss chairs while Baby tries to speak.)*
Baby:	*(Loudly, in frustration.)* EXCUSE ME!
Ma/Pa:	*(Together.)* WHAT?
Baby:	Somebody has been sitting in my chair AND BROKE IT!

Pa:	Maybe we should go look in our bedroom. *(All exit, then return.)*
Ma:	Land sakes, Pa, you don't think someone was in our bedroom.
Baby:	Excuse me ... *(Tries to speak but is interrupted.)*
Pa:	Somebody has been sleeping in my bed!
Baby:	Excuse me … *(Tries to speak but is interrupted.)*
Ma:	Somebody has been sleeping in my bed! *(Ma and Pa discuss while Baby tries to speak.)*
Baby:	*(In exasperation.)* EXCUSE ME!
Ma/Pa:	*(Together.)* WHAT!
Baby:	Somebody has been sleeping in my bed, AND SHE'S STILL THERE!!! *(Triceralocks appears and screeches; all characters tumble around.)*
Triceralocks:	Oh my goodness! Three saber-tooth bears! I'm going to be eaten! What big teeth you have!
Pa:	Relax, child, that's a different fairy tale.
Ma:	Why, we don't eat little girls, we only eat fern flakes. What's your name, child?
Triceralocks:	Mmmmmy name is Triceralocks. Are you s-sure you don't eat little girls?
Pa:	Never.
Ma:	Never.
Baby:	Never.
Triceralocks:	I was out walking, and I got lost, and then I found your place, and the fern flakes smelled so good, and ...
Ma:	Relax, child, why don't I make some more fern flakes and we'll all sit down and have some breakfast.
Baby:	Excuse me … *(Tries to speak but is interrupted.)*
Pa:	That sounds like a fine idea, Ma. *(Ma and Pa discuss as Baby tries to speak.)*
Baby:	EXCUSE ME!
Ma/Pa:	*(Together.)* WHAT!
Baby:	We only have three bowls. *(Everybody groans.)*
	Music (approx. 15 seconds).

Reptile—Color and mount on cardboard. Attach a string or stick to move across stage.

Stable Fella

A Western Twist on "Cinderella"

(My thanks to Jody Harding for this story.)

■▪■▪■▪■▪■▪■▪■▪■▪■▪■▪■▪■▪■▪■▪■▪■▪■

Number of Puppets: 8	**Props:**
• Stable Fella	• Haystack
• Dan (the stepfather)	• Pitchfork
• Luke (the stepbrother)	• Shiny cowboy hat
• Duke (the other stepbrother)	• Shiny cowboy boots
• Rodeo Princess	• Loose hay
• Fairy Hogfather	**Setting:** Farmyard
• White Horse	**Lighting:** No special effects
• Pig	**Music:** Country music
Playing Time: 15–20 minutes	

Scene 1

Action:	*Music (approx. 20 seconds). Haystack on corner of stage, Stable Fella is asleep against it.*
Stable Fella:	*(Snoring, then speaks in his sleep.)* Yawn! I'm soooo tired after working such a long day … *(Snores.)* Yes ma'am … 2+2 is 4 … 4+4 is … *(Snores.)* Of course I'm the sheriff … Look at this tin star …
Dan:	*(Enters.)* Stable Fella! Where is that good for nothin' varmint? Blast it! Stable Fella!
Stable Fella:	*(Wakens with a start.)* Yipes! I musta slept through the plowin'! Big Bad Dan is gonna be ornery! *(To Dan.)* Commin' Sah!
Dan:	*(Condescending.)* Hey Stable Fella … Where you been all day? Was you sleepun'? No sweet potato pie for you t'night. Now get back to that haystack … you got 10 piles that big tomorrow. GET TO WORK! Or I'll lay a thumpin' on ya. *(Exits.)*
	(Enter Luke and Duke.)
Luke:	Stable, do me a favor. I need my hoss to be ready for tomorrow, for the Rodeo Hoedown! And I'm gonna win a dance with the Rodeo Princess! And after you've bathed my hoss you can wash my best shirt and bolo tie! Haha! I reckon you'll even dust off my chaps and rebraid a bullwhip for me!

Duke:	Yeah right. You're dreamin' polecat! I'm gonna win and be her cowboy. No amount of cleanin' will get the stink out of your chaps, Luke. Now Stable Fella, I'm gonna need you to make me a big western sandwich, and a can o' baked beans. I gotta big day tomorrow, and a man can't become Rodeo Prince on an empty belly. An' after that I need you to milk the cows, 'cause I can't do it on account of me being the future Rodeo Prince. See you after the rodeo, Stable Fella. And by the way, you can't come. Wouldn't want common folk like you to be messin' up this affair.
Dan:	*(Enters.)* Boys! I overheard down at the saloon that there's some kinda Rodeo Hoedown. You thinkin' on enterin'? *(Duke and Luke nod.)* Well ain't that a kick in the pants! I know at least one of you is destined for greatness. I'll take you down in the chuckwagon, and we can gets some fancy eats before we settle down and win the prize.
Stable Fella:	Gee, Duke … maybe I shouldn't cook that omelet …
Duke:	Quiet now! I'll need somethin' to warm my stomach up before I feast.
Luke:	Hah hah! Like you need any more fillin'!
Dan:	Both of you shoosh. We need to get ready. Stable Fella … I need the chores done twice as good as usual, and instead of 10 piles of hay this time, I have eight piles …
Stable Fella:	*(To audience.)* Phew! Well, at least it isn't as much as …
Dan:	Stable Fella, listen up, you're daydreamin' again. I want eight piles of manure behind the barn. So pick up a shovel and get shovelin'. *(To Duke, Luke.)* I need you two to help me with my harnesses … c'mon!
	(Dan exits; Luke and Duke follow.)
Duke:	*(As he goes.)* Later, shovel–boy.
Stable Fella:	Manure? Eww! How am I gonna get to the rodeo? I really wish I could go to it … but there's not enough time … what will I do? *(Exits.)*

Scene 2

Action:	*Music (approx. 15 seconds). Stable Fella asleep on stage, snoring.*
Stable Fella:	*(Snoring louder and shifting.)* Yes Ma … I'll deliver the milk to Mr. … *(Toss and snore.)* Yes … I am a trapeze artist … *(Snoring even louder.)* Why yes Miss Rodeo Princess … I'd love to line dance with you … *(Stable Fella awakens.)* What the? What's that noise?

Hogfather:	Wahh-hooooo!!!! Eeeeeeeeeeee … *(Enters on pig, hurtling in from stage right, nearly missing Stable, and into the haystack. Hay flies in air; Hogfather coughs.)* Hoo-haah. Hog! Ease up on the speed next time!
Stable Fella:	Holy cow! Are you okay mister?
Hogfather:	*(Shaking himself off.)* Mystical pig!
Stable Fella:	Pardon?
Hogfather:	My mount is most definitely a mystical pig. I'll have none of your holy cow business!
Stable Fella:	Who are you?
Hogfather:	I am, most definitely, your very own Fairy Hogfather! I hear you're having problems with your stepfather and his sons … what can I do for you?
Stable Fella:	I'm sorry … I just woke up … what is it you do again?
Hogfather:	I am a magical pig farmer from three counties over. I also grant wishes. Now what is your wish? There's a bowler in *(provide place name)* who wished for a lucky strike and I don't have much time to spare. Heh heh.
Stable Fella:	Well …. If I were to wish for somethin' I'd wish to be the Rodeo Prince at the big hoedown tonight! But … I have soooo many chores … and even if I got them done right now, I'd not have any clothes to wear … just my dirty, smelly farmhand clothes …
Hogfather:	Don't you worry your little head. I'll need some ingredients for this wish to work though …. I'm gonna need some hay, some manure … a donkey and a western sandwich … you know, with egg and cheese and peppers? Yeah … that should be about it. Can you get me those things?
Stable Fella:	Are you sure you can help me? I don't put much credence in you snake oil guys trying to sell me stuff.
Hogfather:	Sell? This is a gift, you little cowpoke. What are Fairy Hogfathers for? And it'll work if you just get me those ingredients … so scoot! *(Exits.)*
Stable Fella:	*(Nods.)* Yes sir. *(Exits.)*

Scene 3

Action:	*Music (approx. 15 seconds). Hogfather onstage next to haystack.*
Stable Fella:	*(Enters.)* Well, I gave all the stuff to you … what did you do with it?

Hogfather:	Well, with the hay, manure, and some magic dust … I made you a new hat, and a nice pair of genuine spur-studded, pointy-toed cowboy boots! *(Puts boots and hat on stage, looks around.)* Where'd I put that donkey?
Stable Fella:	I saw it wander off down the road …. I'll go get it. *(Exits.)*
	(From offstage.) I have him. Now, what are you gonna do with him?
Hogfather:	Well … how about this? YAAAHH! *(Races offstage, donkey sounds are heard, then horse sounds, more hay is thrown, then White Horse races through haystack and appears onstage.)*
Stable Fella:	*(Enters, looks at Horse.)* Wow. That's the most beautiful white horse I've ever seen! How'd you do that?
Hogfather:	You'd be surprised what you'd find in a haystack when you aren't looking for a needle. Heh heh. So there. That's about all you need! You got new duds … and a new hoss … what else could you need?
Stable Fella:	Well, if I have everything … what was the western sandwich for?
Hogfather:	Yeah … that was delicious. Thanks. I was famished! So, there ya go. Now after the hoedown, you gotta come straight home, lickity split, 'cause all those ingredients become ingredients again … and you don't want that happenin' in the middle of a do-si-do, now do ya?
Stable Fella:	Thanks, Godfather.
Hogfather:	Hogfather.
Stable Fella:	Hogfather. Say … it's getting late, how in tarnation am I gonna get there on time before the dancin' begins?
Hogfather:	You sell me short, pokey. This here is a mystical horse. It'll get you there in no time. It's a more recent model than the one I ride, so it should get you there in minutes! I've been thinkin' of trading in my pig power for some horsepower! *(Pig squeals.)* Sorry, just jokin' you. Well, I'm off, Stable Fella. Have fun bein' the Rodeo Prince! *(Exits.)*
Stable Fella:	Yeah, see ya … you'll come back now ya hear? Got my new duds. Got my magic powered horse. And got a good chance at this hoedown. *(Gets on Horse.)* This is it then. Yaaah! *(Horse rears and both race offstage.)*

Scene 4

Action:	*Music (approx. 15 seconds). At dance. Dan, Luke, and Duke onstage.*
Dan:	Well boys, we're here. What do y'all want to do?

Duke:	I'm gonna go and enter the steak-eatin' contest. The Rodeo Princess will surely like a man who can appreciate a good meal! I'll eat my way to her heart.
Luke:	EWW. That's gross and revoltin'. I'm gonna show her my roping skills. That way I can show her how much of a cowboy I really am!
Dan:	I'm sure you young 'uns will have her runnin' round like a chicken with her head cut off over both of ya. I'm gonna go watch the livestock show, maybe pick up some choice cattle. Good luck boys.
	(All exit.)

Scene 5

Action:	*Music (approx. 15 seconds). At dance.*
Stable Fella:	*(Enters on Horse.)* Aaaiiieeee! Woaaaah Horsey! Woah! *(Horse comes to a stop.)* Holey moley! You're a fast horse. Okay … let's get on with it. *(Dismounts, and Horse trots offstage.)* You come back when I call, I may be rushed on account of me tryin' to get close enough to talk to the Rodeo Princess! Wish me luck! *(Walks a few steps and looks around.)*
Princess:	*(Enters opposite side, sighs.)* This is a terrible day! None of the cowboys are worth their salt ….
Stable Fella:	*(Looks at Princess.)* Hi lady. Do you know where the Rodeo Princess would be? I'm s'posed to meet her and be her Rodeo Prince. See? I got my fanciest hat, a shiny new white horse nearby, and these *(kicks a leg into the air)*—my spur-studded, pointy-toed cowboy boots! Purty keen huh?
Princess:	Yeah, they are quite nice. Say, what's your name, cowboy?
Stable Fella:	Stab … Steven! My name is Steven. *(To audience.)* Gee, she's awful pretty isn't she? Maybe I should ask this lady to dance … it'll be forever before I find the Rodeo Princess. *(To Princess.)* How has your day been?
Princess:	Nice to meet you, Steven. *(Aside, to audience.)* If this feller dances as well as he looks, I think I might have found my Rodeo Prince! *(To Stable.)* Well, it's been pretty slow. A lot of the cowpokes here want to dance with me … but none of them tickle my fancy. For instance, the last two. One of them nearly hanged me with his silly rope tricks, the other one just sat at a table and ate and ate and ate, then he got sick. I think I like you, though. Can you dance?
Stable Fella:	I can definitely try!
Princess:	Well, lets mosey on out to the hoedown then! *(Music—Stable and Princess dance together.)*

Stable Fella:	I gotta say, you're the purrty-est cowgirl here. And you dance really well too … what was your name? I forgot to ask.
Princess:	Why, thank you. You're not so bad yourself! I'm the Rodeo Princess. And I think you'd make a dandy Rodeo Prince, Steven.
Male Voice:	*(Offstage.)* ATTENTION! The Rodeo Hoedown is now at a close! Take your partners and mosey on home! You can stick around awhile, but we're closin' the barn doors soon! G'night!
Stable Fella:	Oh no! I gotta go, Princess! I'm sorry, but I'm late! *(Whistles.)* HORSE!!! *(Enter Horse. Stable jumps on, leaves behind a boot, and tears off.)*
Princess:	Oh no! He didn't say where he lived! *(Looks around.)* Hey, you left your boot behind!!! Well, now I have somethin' to find him with … whoever has the same spur-studded, pointy-toed cowboy boots is my man!

Scene 6

Action:	*Music (approx. 15 seconds). Haystack on stage, Stable is lying against it.*
Luke:	*(Entering.)* Hey Stable! You missed a good show last night! We saw the Rodeo Princess right after the hoedown, she was awful purrty.
Duke:	*(Entering.)* Yeah, it was a shame … but she wouldn't have even noticed you anyway … she liked us but couldn't decide.
Stable Fella:	I'm sorry I missed it. *(Luke and Duke exit.)*
Princess:	*(Enters.)* Excuse me? I'm looking for a mister Steven … he has spur-studded, pointy-toed cowboy boots. He ran off before I could make him my Rodeo Prince.
Stable Fella:	I … I'm …
Dan:	*(Entering while speaking.)* Quick and clean! Where were you last night? I came back early and found all the chores done and done well. *(To Princess.)* Can I help you, ma'am?
Princess:	Yes sir, I'm looking for a man named Steven ….
Dan:	The only ones here are my sons, Luke an' Duke, and my farmhand, Stable Fella. Say hi, Stable, where are your manners? What's that on your foot, boy?
Stable Fella:	Hey! It's one of my new boots! I musta dropped one on the way home…
Dan:	HOME?! HOME FROM WHERE?! You're mud, Stable Fella!

Princess: No, he isn't. He's my Steven, my Rodeo Prince. Let's ride off into the noon sun, Princey? What do you say?

Stable Fella: Here's what I say! YEEEEE HAAAAWWWWW!

   (Princess and Stable run offstage.)

Dan: But! Who'll do the … and who will make my …?

Hogfather: *(Barrels onstage.)* AAAiiiiEEEEEEEee! *(Crashes into Dan, and both plow into the haystack.)*

   Music (approx. 15 seconds).

Jungle Jack and the Vinestalk

A Jungle Twist on "Jack and the Beanstalk"

■_■_■_■_■_■_■_■_■_■_■_■_■_■_■_■

Number of Puppets: 7

- Jack
- Mama
- Snake
- Man
- Ape (commercial stuffed toy)
- Bird
- Banana

Note: Wife of Ape is voice only; no puppet is necessary

Playing Time: 15–20 minutes

Props:

- Movable vinestalk
- Golden egg (small plastic egg)
- Fire (can be made from cardboard)
- coconuts (Styrofoam balls with shredded brown tissue paper
- flower pods (small bag)

Setting: Jungle scene, small house nearby

Lighting: No special effects

Music: Jungle music

Scene 1

Action:	*Music (approx. 20 seconds). Jungle scene, mother onstage.*
Mama:	Now where is dat Jack? He's never around when I need him. *(Calling.)* Jack, oh JACK! *(Enter Jack, swinging from vine, crashes into tree.)*
	Oh Jack! Come on, pick yourself up now. I've got de job for you to do.
Jack:	A job! Cool man! *(Calling.)* Hey Brownie! C'mon out, Dude, we've got a job! *(Enter Snake.)* So, what's the job, Mama?
Mama:	You goin' to take dat snake to de market to sell it.
Jack:	*(Gasps. Snake wraps itself around him and begins shaking.)* Oh, Mama, you can't! Not Brownie!
Mama:	*(In menacing tone.)* JACK!
Jack:	Bummer. All right, c'mon Brownie. *(Struggle ensues as Jack tries to lead Snake offstage.)*
Mama:	Make sure you get good price, 'cause 'dell cheat you if dey can.
Jack:	Chill, Mama, it'll be cool.

Scene 2

Action: *Music (approx. 15 seconds). Jack is struggling with Snake down jungle path.*

Jack: C'mon, Brownie! It does not do you any good to fight it. *(Snake starts to cry.)* Now Brownie *(sniffs)*, don't get me going. *(Sniffs loudly. Snake sobs loudly. Jack and Snake sob loudly together.)*

Man: *(Enters, carrying flower pods.)* Good morning, Jack.

Jack: *(Sniffing.)* Ya, man. *(Suddenly jumps up.)* How did you know my name?

Man: Oh, that's not important. Listen, I heard you're selling your snake. *(Snake immediately hides behind Jack.)*

Jack: *(Sadly.)* Ya, man.

Man: Well, I'll trade you your snake for these flower pods.

Jack: G'wan man! Dis is not a deal.

Man: Oh, but these are magic flower pods. If you plant them at night, by morning you'll have a vinestalk right up to the sky.

Jack: *(Pausing.)* Well, alright. *(To Snake.)* So long ol' bud.

Man: Thank you, Jack. You won't regret this. Come along, Brownie. *(Snake struggles and sobs loudly, makes choking sounds, wraps around tree, etc. Man pulls snake off and exits with Snake. Jack slowly walks off.)*

Scene 3

Action: *Music (approx. 15 seconds). Back at home. Mama is waiting. Jack enters.*

Mama: Bless me, Jack. You have been quick. You haven't got de snake, so I guess you sell her. How much you get for her?

Jack: *(Pausing.)* Uh, dis one you'll not guess.

Mama: Good boy! Five dollar? Ten dollar?

Jack: I tell you you'll not guess. I trade Brownie for de flower pods.

Mama: Whaaa?

Jack: De flower pods, Mama. Dey magic.

Mama: *(Plaintively.)* Magic? Oh, Jack. Deez pods is no good. I might as well throw dem. Yes, right out de window. Now put yourself to bed, Jack. *(Exit Mama and Jack.)*

Scene 4

Action: *Music (approx. 15 seconds). Vinestalk grows. Enter Jack.*

Jack: Man, what a dream I had. *(Sees vinestalk, jumps back in surprise.)* Oh man! It wasn't a dream! De flower pods, dey were magic! *(Looks up, examines stalk.)* I suppose I got ta climb up de vinestalk now. Well, here goes ….

Scene 5

Action: *Music (approx. 15 seconds). Jack reaches top of vinestalk.*

Jack: Woa! So dis is de top of de vinestalk. *(Hears loud banging.)* Oh man, something big is comin'. It's a GIANT! A giant GORILLA! *(Jack hides.)*

Ape: Wife! Where's my breakfast! Where's my banana porridge!

Wife: *(Offstage.)* Enough already with the porridge! It's coming! Hold on to your patooties!

Ape: Mmmm, I can smell it *(sniffs)*. But what's this? *(Ape sniffs around while Jack hides.)*

Fe-fi-fo-fid
I smell the scent of a jungle kid
If I catch him, and indeed I hope
I'll scrub him all over
with water and soap!

Jack: *(Gasping quietly.)* A bath? Oh no man, not de bath!

Wife: *(Offstage.)* Would you relax! Why don't you count your coconuts while you're waiting for breakfast? *(Place large chest onstage.)*

Ape: Oooohh, oooohh. Yea! Ooooh. My coconuts. *(Looks in chest)* 1 … 2 … 3 … *(starts to nod)* 4 … 5 … 6 … zzzzz *(snores loudly)*.

Jack: Oh man, coconuts! We could eat well at home. If I just get da chest. *(Jack tries to take chest from ape, has several close calls, then takes chest down the vinestalk.)*

Scene 6

Action: *Music (approx. 15 seconds). At home. Mama is looking for Jack.*

Mama: Now where did dat Jack go now?

Jack:	*(Calling from afar.)* Look out below! *(Coconuts start falling. Mama screams. Jack arrives with chest.)* I tell you, Mama, dey were magic flower pods. Dat vinestalk grew from dem. I climbed it and found a giant gorilla. Big guy—oooohh, oooohh, oooohh. When he go to sleep, I take da coconuts!
Mama:	Oh Jack. I don' know what I do without you … I don' know what I do with you, either! *(Exit together.)*

■▄■▄■▄■▄■▄■▄■▄■▄■▄■▄■▄■▄■▄■▄■▄■▄■▄

Scene 7

Action:	*Music (approx. 15 seconds). Jack is alone at house.*
Jack:	Coconut is gone, man. I have to take another trip up de vinestalk. Maybe dat giant gorilla got more of de coconut. *(Music, starts to climb.)* Oh man, de top of de vinestalk again. But I don' see any of de coconuts. *(Hears loud banging.)* Oh man, it's dat big gorilla again, an I don' want a bath! *(Hides.)*
Ape:	Wife! Where's my dinner! Where's my fruit salad?
Wife:	*(Offstage.)* Keep your knickers on! It's coming!
Ape:	Mmmm. I love the smell of fresh fruit salad … the pineapples … *(sniffs)* the kiwi *(sniffs)* the … *(sniffs)* … DIRTY BOY!

Fe-fi-fo-fid
I smell the scent of a jungle kid
If I catch him, and indeed I hope
I'll scrub him all over
with water and soap. |
| **Jack:** | *(Quietly.)* Oh no, man, not de bath. |
| **Wife:** | Enough already with that fe-fi-fo foolishness. Here! *(Bird comes on stage.)* Take care of the bird. |
| **Ape:** | *(Grumbling.)* Silly-looking bird. Come on bird—lay a golden egg. *(Bird looks at him, cocking head. Ape talks sweetly.)* Come on, lay an egg for Daddy. *(Ape strokes Bird, Bird pecks ape.)* Why you rotten bird! Fine! You won't lay, I'll squeeze the egg out of you! *(Struggle ensues, large egg is produced.)*

Plum tuckered me out, you did. I think I'll have a little nap before dinner. *(Yawns and starts to snore. Bird backs up to exit, clucking softly—backs into Jack. Loud cluck, Ape stirs.)* |
| **Jack:** | Shhh! You got ta be quiet, bird. I'm not in de mood for a bath, and I don't think you want de stuffing squeezed out of you again. *(Bird responds.)* C'mon, man, come on down de vinestalk with me. *(Music, both climb down.)* |

■▄■▄■▄■▄■▄■▄■▄■▄■▄■▄■▄■▄■▄■▄■▄■▄■▄

Scene 8

Action:　*Music (approx. 15 seconds). Mama is outside, looking for Jack.*

Mama:　Now where is dat boy of mine now?

Jack:　*(Calling from afar.)* Look out below! *(Bird clucks loudly and giant egg falls. Mama screams. Jack and Bird arrive on stage.)* Mama, I've been up de vinestalk again. Dis time I got … *(pauses, turns to Bird).* I'm sorry, I didn't catch your name. *(Bird clucks.)* Mama, dis is *(imitates Bird).* She lays golden eggs.

Mama:　Jack, my boy, you never cease to amaze me. Give your mama a big hug. *(Jack and Mama hug, Bird joins in, all exit.)*

Scene 9

Action:　*Music (approx. 15 seconds). Jack by vinestalk.*

Jack:　Well, man, it's time for another trip up de vinestalk. De golden eggs, dey were great, but when de bird find out what we done to Brownie … well, she took off. Can't say that I blame her. Well, here goes …. *(Music—Jack goes up vinestalk.)*

Scene 10

Action:　*Music (approx. 15 seconds). Jack at top of vinestalk.*

Jack:　Ya man, here again. *(Looks around.)* No coconuts … no birds … hmmm. I wonder what else dat big gorilla got. *(Hears loud banging.)* Oh man, here he comes again. I'd better hide!

Ape:　Wife! Where's my supper! Where's my fried mangoes?

Wife:　*(Offstage.)* Don't get your underwear in a knot! It's coming!

Ape:　Mmmm. The smell of fried mangoes. *(Sniffs.)* It's enough to … *(sniffs)* … wait a minute! *(long sniff)*

Fe-fi-fo-fid
I smell the scent of a jungle kid
If I catch him, and indeed I hope
I'll scrub him all over
with water and soap.

Jack:　*(Quietly.)* No man, not de bath.

Wife:　Stop that fe-fi-fo foolishness or you'll be wearing your supper. Why don't you listen to some music?

Ape:	Good idea. WIFE. Bring me my singing banana! *(Banana comes on stage)* Well … SING! Sing something lively, sing about … ME! *(Music—theme song from* The Monkees. *Banana sings, Ape dances.)*
	Whew! That one wore me right out. I think I'll take a little nap. Come here, Banana, I need a pillow. *(Ape curls up with Banana and starts to snore.)*
Jack:	*(Approaching cautiously.)* Come with me, Banana, we'll make beautiful music together. Careful … we don't want to wake de big guy. *(Jack starts to move Banana and Ape rolls over. Banana is free, but Jack is caught.)* Oh man, dis is not a good plan. *(Jack tries to wriggle free. Ape finally rolls over and Jack is free. Music— "Rescue Me." Ape wakes up.)*
Ape:	Oh, you smelly little jungle boy. I'll get you! *(Chase ensues and all run offstage.)*

Scene 11

Action:	*Music (approx. 15 seconds). Jack and Banana come down stalk, Banana is singing loudly.*
Jack:	Mama! Come quick! *(To Banana.)* Quiet, man! Mama, come get de fire going under de vinestalk. De big gorilla is coming! Hurry, Mama! *(Mama enters and sets up fire.)*
Ape:	*(At vinestalk.)* I'll get you, you smelly little varmint! I'll … *(touches fire)*. Ooohh, Ooohh, that's hot! Eeee, Eeee! *(Starts back up vinestalk.)*
Jack:	Well, I guess dat's de last we see of de big gorilla. C'mon Mama, let's go home.
	Music (suggestion: "Daylight Come and Me Wanna Go Home," approx. 15 seconds. Banana sings, and all exit.)

Rumpled Turkey

A Thanksgiving Twist on "Rumpelstiltskin"

■□■□■□■□■□■□■□■□■□■□■□■□■□■□■□■

Number of Puppets: 5

- King (rather unattractive)
- Miller
- Daughter
- Rumpled Turkey (with cape)
- Clementine Turkey (rather unattractive, with heavy veil)

Playing Time: 15–20 minutes

Props:

- Small loaf of bread
- Small plate of cookies,
- Talcum powder (to throw as flour)
- Spoon
- Pots and pans (to rattle offstage)

Setting: Inside Royal Castle

Lighting: No special effects

Music: Music depicting royalty: trumpets, etc.

Scene 1

Action:	*Music (approx. 20 seconds). Inside Royal Castle. King is onstage.*
King:	*(Groaning.)* Oooooh, if I hear one more boasting peasant I think I shall scream. Really! Some of these people just carry on so! The last one bragged he could find a unicorn for me, while the one before that said that he could turn straw into gold. Now that's ridiculous! I must do something about this. The stories are getting more and more outlandish. *(Knock at door.)*
	(To audience.) What's this? Another one? *(Calls loudly.)* Enter!
Miller:	*(Enters.)* Your Majesty. *(Bows.)*
King:	Yes, Miller, what can I do for you?
Miller:	As a servant of Your Majesty, I present you with this very fine loaf of bread. I milled the flour for it myself, and my daughter baked it especially for you.
King:	Why, thank you, Miller. That is a fine-looking loaf of bread. *(Tastes bread.)* Mmmm. This is delicious! Best I've had in ages. I wish I had a wife who could cook like this. And with Thanksgiving coming … what I wouldn't give for a home-cooked turkey dinner.
Miller:	Turkey dinner? Why, my daughter makes the best turkey dinner in this kingdom.

King:	*(Skeptical.)* Oh, really?
Miller:	Not only this kingdom, but all the kingdoms far and near.
King:	*(To audience.)* Here we go again. Another one bragging to the King. *(To Miller.)* Well, if your daughter can make a turkey dinner as well as she bakes bread, I'll ask for her hand in marriage. But I'll warn you, Miller. If you are lying to me about your daughter, I will have you thrown in the dungeon.
Miller:	The dungeon! Well, actually, Your Majesty, my daughter really …
King:	Enough! Bring your daughter here tomorrow. We shall see about her skills in the kitchen.
Miller:	Yyyes, Your Majesty. *(Bows.)*
	(To audience.) What have I done? *(Exits.)*
King:	Hmmm. A fine turkey dinner. Well, that sounds a little more promising than spinning straw into gold. Let's see how the little lady does tomorrow. *(Exits.)*

Scene 2

Action:	*Music (approx. 15 seconds). Miller's house. Miller and Daughter are discussing visit to King.*
Miller:	I have wonderful news for you, my dear. Tomorrow you will meet the King!
Daughter:	Don't be silly, Father. I don't want to meet the King.
Miller:	*(Bursts into fitful sobs.)* But you have to. If you don't go, the King will lock me in the dungeon!
Daughter:	The dungeon! What kind of a cruel man would lock you in the dungeon for nothing?
Miller:	*(Softly sobbing.)* It wasn't really nothing …. Well, it wasn't really something … it was … really a little something of nothing … it was …
Daughter:	*(Controlling her anger.)* What did you tell him, Father?
Miller:	*(Sobbing loudly.)* I told him you could make the best turkey dinner in all the kingdoms, near and far!
Daughter:	But Father, I can't make the King a royal turkey dinner. I can't even cook! You know that. You do all the cooking around here. You should be making the turkey dinner.

Miller:	Maybe I should, Daughter, but I don't think the King wants to marry me. Besides, once he see how beautiful you are, and how well you sew and clean about the house, he'll surely fall in love with you.
Daughter:	*(Dreamily.)* Is the King handsome, Father?
Miller:	Well, he's rather … actually, he's a bit on the …
Daughter:	Never mind, Father. I think I don't want to know. I'll go to the castle tomorrow. Maybe I can explain to the King that there was a slight misunderstanding.

Scene 3

Action:	*Music (approx. 15 seconds). King's castle, in the kitchen. King is onstage; Daughter enters.*
King:	Good day to you, my beautiful lady. You must be the Miller's daughter.
Daughter:	*(To audience.)* Yuck! *(To King.)* Good day, your hands … handso … *(To audience.)* Oh, I can't! *(Bows to King.)* Good day, your Majesty.
King:	Thank you for the delicious bread you baked for me yesterday.
Daughter:	The bread I baked for you?
King:	Yes, quite splendid it was. Your father tells me that you make the finest turkey dinner in all the kingdoms put together.
Daughter:	Well, that's not exactly so. You see, I can't even …
King:	Yes, yes, I know. Famous chefs are always quit modest about their creations. Here you are, my dear. We shall have a sampling of your fabulous cooking. Make me another loaf of bread. I will return in a few hours. If you have accomplished the deed when I return, we will discuss marriage. If you have not, your father will be thrown in the dungeon for lying. *(Exits.)*
Daughter:	Marry him? *(Shudders.)* Eeeugh. *(Softly.)* Oh, help. *(Pause, then slightly louder.)* Oh, help. *(Pause, then very loud.)* OH, HELP!
Turkey:	*(Offstage.)* Have no fear, Rumpled Turkey is here!
Daughter:	*(To audience.)* What was that?!?
Turkey:	*(Still offstage, loud crashes are heard.)* Nope, not this room … *(another crash and a scream).* Sorry Lady … AHA! *(Turkey flies in, knocking Daughter over.)*
Daughter:	*(Groaning, gets up.)* Who are you?
Turkey:	Didn't you hear me coming?

Daughter:	Of course I heard you coming. Half of the kingdom heard you coming!
Turkey:	Yes, well, my landings need a little practice. *(Pause.)* As to who I am … *(clears throat, then yells).* RUMPLED TURKEY TO THE RESCUE! I'm your average, ordinary superhero, of the poultry variety. Now, what seems to be the trouble?
Daughter:	I'm supposed to bake a loaf of bread for the King, and I'm hopeless at cooking!
Turkey:	*(Laughs foolishly.)* Is that all? Why, I can whip you up a loaf in no time! I just need to find the ingredients in the pantry. *(Exits—crashing and gobbling heard, flour flies in the air, a spoon flies by. Turkey races onstage, then off.)* Now, to the oven … *(more crashing and gobbling—Turkey returns with loaf of bread, places it on table.)*
Daughter:	Wow! That looks fabulous!
Turkey:	*(Walking toward Daughter.)* All in a superhero's day. Why, just the other day … *(trips and falls on stage).*
Daughter:	Oh! Are you all right?
Turkey:	*(Annoyed.)* I keep tripping on my superhero cape.
Daughter:	I can fix that. I'm very good at sewing, just not so good at baking. *(Reaches around Turkey and sews hem of cape.)* There. You shouldn't have any more troubles with your cape. Oh, I hear the King coming! You'd better go!
Turkey:	*(To audience.)* I can't believe she fixed my cape. Nobody has ever done something like that for me. It's always "Help me, superhero, help me." And then when I help them, they mumble thanks and leave.
Daughter:	You have to leave now! The King is almost here!
Turkey:	*(Sighs.)* Yes, I will go, fair maiden. But first, pray tell me your name.
Daughter:	The King's here! GO! *(Pushes Turkey, King enters and Turkey knocks him over as he leaves.)*
King:	*(Slowly getting up.)* What was that?
Daughter:	Oh, it must have been the breeze. I like to keep the windows open when I cook. It gets rather hot.
King:	Yes, well, let's taste that delicious bread of yours. I could smell it all the way down the hall. *(Samples bread.)* Mmmm. This is delicious! It has a different texture though. Some special ingredient, perhaps? What's this? A feather in the bread?
Daughter:	*(To audience.)* Hmm, I'd better think fast. *(To King.)* Yes, I throw in a few feathers to make the bread fluffier. You know how fluffy a down pillow is.

| King: | I never would have thought of that! Come, my dear, let's go for a walk in the courtyard. *(King and Daughter exit.)* |

Scene 4

Action:	*Music (approx. 15 seconds). Back in King's kitchen. King and Daughter are onstage.*
King:	Lovely walk, my dear. How about making us some delicious cookies to snack on?
Daughter:	Oh no! Er, I mean I'm still full from the bread. Wouldn't you rather wait a while for …
King:	Wait a while? For your delicious baking? Why, I can't get enough of it. How about some chocolate chip cookies? I'll come back in an hour or so. *(Exits.)*
Daughter:	Here we go again. I can't bake cookies. *(Softly.)* Oh, help. *(Pause, then slightly louder.)* Oh, help. *(Pause, then very loud.)* OH, HELP!
Turkey:	*(Offstage.)* Have no fear, Rumpled Turkey is here!
Daughter:	*(To audience.)* Did you hear that? Do you suppose?
Turkey:	*(Still offstage, loud crashes heard.)* Nope, not here *(another crash and an angry voice yelling)* … pardon me … now where was that room … AHA! *(Turkey flies in, knocking Daughter over.)*
Daughter:	*(Groaning, gets up.)* I hoped you would come back, but I was hoping you would come back a little quieter.
Turkey:	Can't do that, lady. A superhero always yells. *(Clears throat, then yells.)* RUMPLED TURKEY TO THE RESCUE! *(Makes gobbling sounds, flaps wings, and struts around stage.)*
Daughter:	Shhh. Quiet! The King thinks I'm up here alone.
Turkey:	What is the trouble, fair maiden?
Daughter:	*(To audience.)* Fair maiden? *(To Turkey.)* Yes, well, the King wants me to bake some chocolate chip cookies, and, well, I can't bake any better than the last time I met you. *(Pause.)* I was hoping that …
Turkey:	*(Laughs foolishly.)* Yes, yes, you were hoping that I could whip you up some delicious cookies. Easier than bread, my dear. I'll just zip into the pantry again … *(Exits—crashing and gobbling heard. Flour flies by, mixing sounds, spoon flies by. Turkey races onstage then off.)* Now to the oven … *(more crashing and gobbling heard—Turkey returns with a plate of cookies).*

Daughter:	Wow! They look terrific!
Turkey:	Try one.
Daughter:	*(Sampling cookie.)* Mmmm. This is delicious! If only I could bake even half as good as you …
Turkey:	If only I could sew half as good as you …
Daughter:	We make a good team, don't we? *(Looking)* You are kind of cute … and … oh, you have a button loose on your cape. Just give me a minute, and I'll have that fixed right up. *(Sews button back on cape.)* There!
Turkey:	*(To audience.)* I can't believe it! She did it again! I didn't even ask for help and she …
Daughter:	I hear the King … you'd better go!
Turkey:	*(Still to audience.)* A button this time. Last time was the cape, and this time …
Daughter:	You really have to go now! The King is almost here!
Turkey:	*(Sighs.)* Yes, I will go, fair maiden. But first, your name …
Daughter:	The King is here! GO! *(Pushes Turkey, King enters and Turkey knocks him over as he leaves.)*
King:	*(Slowly getting up.)* That's some strong breeze up here!
Daughter:	Yes, well, it does inspire me to bake.
King:	And what an excellent baker you are, my dear.
Daughter:	*(To audience.)* Not really.
King:	Well, shall we taste those cookies of yours? My, they smell delicious. Chocolate chip, are they?
Daughter:	Chocolate chip thumbprint cookies, Your Majesty.
King:	Thumbprint cookies, you say? Hmm, it doesn't look like a thumbprint. Funny, it looks more like a bird's footprint.
Daughter:	*(To audience.)* So THAT'S how he flattened the cookies!
King:	Mmmm. These are fabulous! Oh, but you must be exhausted. First, a loaf of bread, and then a plate of chocolate chip thumbprint cookies. You need to rest, my dear. Tomorrow is Thanksgiving, and you will need all your strength to cook me the best turkey dinner I've ever had. And after that, you shall become my wife. Come, my dear, I'll show you to your room. *(Both exit.)*

Scene 5

Action:	*Music (approx. 15 seconds). Back in King's kitchen.*
Daughter:	Oh boy, how am I going to make a turkey dinner for the King? And worse yet, I'm supposed to marry him! Eeeugh. *(Softly.)* Oh, help. *(Pause, then slightly louder.)* Oh, help. *(Pause, then very loud.)* OH, HELP!
Turkey:	*(Flies in, slides past Daughter and offstage into pantry. Pots and pans clatter. Returns on stage, clears throat then speaks softly.)* Have no fear, Rumpled Turkey is here.
Daughter:	*(Pause.)* Well, that was a little better.
Turkey:	I've been practicing.
Daughter:	Keep up the good work.
Turkey:	What seems to be the trouble?
Daughter:	The King wants me to cook him a turkey dinner.
Turkey:	TURKEY DINNER! *(Makes gobbling sounds, flaps around stage, panicking.)*
Daughter:	Oh, I forgot. You're a turkey.
Turkey:	I'M NOT COOKING YOU A TURKEY!
Daughter:	But what am I going to do? If I don't prepare him the best turkey dinner he's ever had, my goose is cooked!
Turkey:	*Your* goose is cooked?
Daughter:	Sorry. *(Pause.)* Oh please, you have to help me.
Turkey:	Well, I am a superhero. *(Pause, thinking.)* Tell you what … I'll give you three chances to guess my name, and if you do, I'll help you with dinner.
Daughter:	Um, Rumpled Turkey?
Turkey:	Drat! That one never works on me! Well, I guess it's my goose who's cooked!
Daughter:	Not so fast, I have an idea. *(Whispers to Turkey.)*
Turkey:	Hmmm … uh ha … yes! That just might do it! Let's get started! *(Both exit.)*

■▪■▪■▪■▪■▪■▪■▪■▪■▪■▪■▪■▪■▪■▪■▪■▪

Scene 6

Action:	*Music (approx. 15 seconds). King and Daughter onstage in kitchen.*

King:	Outstanding meal, my dear. The sweet potatoes were scrumptious … the cranberries were cooked to perfection … the pumpkin pie was delectable … and the turkey … wait a minute, where was the turkey?
Daughter:	The turkey? Why he was out here with me, Your Majesty. You see, my turkey dinner is very special in that it requires a turkey to help me cook it.
King:	Hmmm. *(Looking around.)* And where is he now?
Daughter:	He's doing the dishes. *(Banging and gobbling heard in background.)*
King:	*(Laughing.)* Well, I never heard of that cooking secret before! Regardless, I have made up my mind. You shall be my Queen tomorrow. *(Exits.)*
Daughter:	Marry him? Ugh. *(Softly.)* Oh, help. *(Pause, then slightly louder.)* Oh, help. *(Turkey walks onstage just as Daughter yells.)* OH, HELP! *(Face each other, Daughter screams, Turkey gobbles.)*
Turkey:	*(Frustrated.)* What's wrong now? The meal is finished, the dishes are done, the …
Daughter:	I have to marry the King.
Turkey:	Marry the King?
Daughter:	Tomorrow.
Turkey:	Eeew. Maybe you'll have to run away and become a superhero like me. That's how I avoided marrying Clementine.
Daughter:	Clementine? Who's Clementine?
Turkey:	Oh, she was a chick I met in my younger days. Our parents arranged a marriage for us.
Daughter:	What happened?
Turkey:	She grew up. Kind of like your King.
Daughter:	Eeew.
Turkey:	Anyways, I ran away. That's how I became *(shouts)* RUMPLED TURKEY, superhero to all.
Daughter:	Listen, superhero, I've got an idea. *(Whispers to Turkey.)*
Turkey:	Hmmm … uh ha … yes! What a plan! Come on, we've got a lot of work to do! *(Both exit.)*

Scene 7

Action: *Music (wedding song, approx. 15 seconds). King is onstage, Clementine comes onstage with a heavy veil, bumping around.*

King: That's quite the veil you have, my dear. Here, let me help you. (*Leads Clementine onstage. More music is played. Voice of Minister is heard.*)

Minister: (*Voice only.*) I now pronounce you man and wife. You may kiss the bride. (*King lifts veil and screams. Clementine gobbles. Both run offstage.*)

Music (approx. 15 seconds).

Making the Puppets

The next step after deciding on a puppet script is to make the puppets. You need to decide what type of puppets are best for your show, and who is going to make the puppets.

Easy Puppets

The easy puppets are all simple hand puppets. They are created by gluing or sewing two pieces of felt together, and are decorated with other pieces of felt. They require little or no sewing abilities, and are very quick to make. Classrooms planning puppet presentations may choose this method of puppet creation as children will have little difficulty making these puppets.

Advanced Puppets

Advanced puppets are considerably more detailed than their simple counterparts. They are created with fun fur, blanket fleece, or other materials, and they require intermediate to advanced sewing skills to create. The main advantage of these puppets is that they are three-dimensional and more realistic in appearance. Many of them are mouth puppets and, for this reason, they allow more dynamic presentations of the puppet shows. Librarians and teachers who are planning to present puppet shows might consider making these puppets, as they create a higher quality performance. For those who are not handy with a sewing machine, consider volunteer workers. Many libraries and schools have talented volunteers available for fun projects such as these.

Getting Started

Instructions and patterns for both easy and advanced methods of puppet creation follow. The easy method is introduced first, and is followed by the advanced method. Choose the method most suited to your needs, and have fun creating!

Note: Because patterns have been reduced to fit on pages, you must enlarge all patterns by 110% on the photocopier before beginning.

Making Easy Puppets

![Easy Person Puppet illustration]

Easy Person Puppet

Pattern Pieces Needed

Easy 1, 2, 7, 8, 9, and 13

Fabric

Felt (flesh-colored, white, black)

Other Materials Needed

Black fabric paint or marker

Instructions

1. Enlarge, copy, and cut out all required paper pattern pieces. Cut two of pattern piece Easy 7. Tape upper body (Easy 1) to lower body (Easy 2) along dotted line. Tape ears (Easy 7) in place. This is the body. Note: One ear is turned backwards.

2. Cut two of the body pattern piece (Easy 1, 2, and 7) from flesh-colored felt.

3. Cut two of eye pattern piece (Easy 8) from white felt.

4. Cut two of pupil pattern piece (Easy 9) from black felt.

5. Cut one of nose pattern piece (Easy 13) from flesh-colored felt.

6. Stitch or glue the body pieces together, leaving bottom open.

7. Glue eyes and pupils into place.

8. Glue nose into place.

9. Draw mouth with fabric paint or marker.

Variations

Boy: Use pattern piece Easy 20 for hair.

Girl: Use pattern piece Easy 21 for hair.

Clothing: Use pattern piece Easy 27 to make vest, shirt, or dress.

King/Prince: Use pattern piece Easy 23 for crown.

Queen/Princess: Use pattern piece Easy 24 for crown.

Jungle Jack/Caveman/Cavewoman: Use pattern piece Easy 25 for clothing.

Stable Fella Characters: Use pattern piece Easy 26 for cowboy hat.

Leprechaun: Use pattern pieces Easy 28 and 29 for hat and pipe.

Troll: Use fun fur for hair; make wild eyes and mouth.

Easy Rabbit Puppet

Pattern Pieces Needed

Easy 1, 2, 6, 8, 9, 12, and 17

Fabric

Felt (brown, beige, white, black, pink)

Other Materials Needed

Black fabric paint or marker

Instructions

1. Enlarge, copy, and cut out all required paper pattern pieces. Cut two of pattern piece Easy 6. Tape upper body (Easy 1) to lower body (Easy 2) along dotted line. Tape ears (Easy 6) in place. This is the body. *Note: One ear is turned backwards.*

2. Cut two of the body pattern piece (Easy 1, 2, and 6) from brown felt.

3. Cut two of eye pattern piece (Easy 8) from white felt.

4. Cut two of pupil pattern piece (Easy 9) from black felt.

5. Cut one of nose pattern piece (Easy 12) from pink felt.

6. Cut two of tooth pattern piece (Easy 17) from white felt.

7. Stitch or glue the body pattern pieces together, leaving bottom open.

8. Glue eyes and pupils into place.

9. Glue nose into place.

10. Draw mouth with fabric paint or marker.

11. Glue teeth into place.

Easy Triceralocks Puppet

Pattern Pieces Needed

Easy 2, 8, 9, 12, 30, 31, and 32

Fabric

Felt (purple, white, black)

Other Materials Needed

Black fabric paint or marker

Instructions

1. Enlarge, copy, and cut out all required paper pattern pieces. Tape upper body (Easy 30) to lower body (Easy 2) along dotted line to create the body.

2. Cut two of the body pattern piece (Easy 2 and 30) from purple felt.

3. Cut two of eye pattern piece (Easy 8) from white felt.

4. Cut two of pupil pattern piece (Easy 9) from black felt.

5. Cut one of nose pattern piece (Easy 12) from black felt.

6. Cut one of horn A pattern piece (Easy 31) from white felt.

7. Cut two of horn B pattern piece (Easy 32) from white felt.

8. Stitch or glue the body pieces together, leaving bottom open.

9. Glue eyes and pupils into place.

10. Glue nose into place.

11. Glue horns into place.

12. Draw mouth with fabric paint or marker.

Easy Ghost Puppet

Pattern Pieces Needed

Easy 1, 2, and 10

Fabric

Felt (black, white)

Instructions

1. Enlarge, copy, and cut out all required paper pattern pieces. Tape upper body (Easy 1) to lower body (Easy 2) along dotted line to create body.

2. Cut two of the body pattern piece (Easy 1 and 2) from white felt.

3. Cut three of eye and mouth pattern piece (Easy 10) from black felt.

4. Stitch or glue the body pieces together, leaving bottom open.

5. Glue eyes and mouth into place.

Easy Pumpkin Puppet

Pattern Pieces Needed

Easy 11, 18, 19, and 33

Fabric

Felt (orange, green, black)

Instructions

1. Enlarge, copy, and cut out all required paper pattern pieces.

2. Cut two of pumpkin pattern piece (Easy 33) from orange felt.

3. Cut three of eye and nose pattern piece (Easy 11) from black felt.

4. Cut one of mouth pattern piece (Easy 18) from black felt.

5. Cut one of stem pattern piece (Easy 19) from green felt.

6. Stitch or glue pumpkin pieces together, leaving bottom open.

7. Glue eyes and nose into place.

8. Glue mouth into place.

9. Glue stem into place.

Easy Saber-tooth Bear Puppet

Pattern Pieces Needed

Easy 1, 2, 4, 8, 9, 12, 15, and 16
Note: You will need to make three different sizes of bears. Use original pattern size for Baby Bear, and enlarge Ma and Pa Bear to desired sizes.

Fabric

Felt (pale-orange, black, white, beige)

Other Materials Needed

Black fabric paint or marker

Instructions

1. Copy and cut out all required paper pattern pieces. Cut two of pattern piece Easy 4. Tape upper body (Easy 1) to lower body (Easy 2) along dotted line. Tape ears (Easy 4) in place. This is the body. *Note: One ear is turned backwards.*

2. Cut two of the body pattern piece (Easy 1, 2, and 4) from pale-orange felt.

3. Cut two of eye pattern piece (Easy 8) from white felt.

4. Cut two of pupil pattern piece (Easy 9) from black felt.

5. Cut one of nose pattern piece (Easy 12) from black felt.

6. Cut one of muzzle pattern piece (Easy 15) from beige felt.

7. Cut two of fang pattern piece (Easy 16) from white felt.

8. Stitch or glue the body pieces together, leaving bottom open.

9. Glue eyes and pupils into place.

10. Glue muzzle into place.

11. Glue nose into place.

12. With fabric paint or marker, draw mouth.

13. Glue fangs into place.

Easy Pig Puppet

Pattern Pieces Needed

Easy 1, 2, 3, 8, 9, 14, and 15

Fabric

Felt (pink, white, black)

Other Materials Needed

Black fabric paint or marker (optional for mouth) pink pipe cleaner (optional for tail)

Instructions

1. Enlarge, copy, and cut out all required paper pattern pieces. Cut two of pattern piece Easy 3. Tape upper body (Easy 1) to lower body (Easy 2) along dotted line. Tape ears (Easy 3) in place. This is the body. *Note: One ear is turned backwards.*

2. Cut two of the body pattern piece (Easy 1, 2 and 3) from pink felt.

3. Cut two of eye pattern piece (Easy 8) from white felt.

4. Cut two of pupil pattern piece (Easy 9) from black felt.

5. Cut two of nostril pattern piece (Easy 14) from black felt.

6. Cut one of muzzle (snout) pattern piece (Easy 15) from pink felt.

7. Stitch or glue the body pieces together, leaving bottom open.

8. Glue eyes and pupils into place.

9. Glue muzzle (snout) and nostrils into place.

Optional: Draw mouth with fabric paint or marker. Glue a pink pipe cleaner for tail.

Easy Horse Puppet

Pattern Pieces Needed

Easy 1, 2, 5, 8, 9, 14, 15, and 22

Fabric

Felt (brown, dark brown, beige, white, black)
Note: Horse in "Stable Fella" is white.

Other Materials Needed

Black fabric paint or marker

Instructions

1. Enlarge, copy, and cut out all required paper pattern pieces. Cut two of pattern piece Easy 5. Tape upper body (Easy 1) to lower body (Easy 2) along dotted line. Tape ears (Easy 5) in place. This is the body. *Note: One ear is turned backwards.*

2. Cut two of the body pattern piece (Easy 1, 2, and 5) from brown felt.

3. Cut two of eye pattern piece (Easy 8) from white felt.

4. Cut two of pupil pattern piece (Easy 9) from black felt.

5. Cut two of nostril pattern piece (Easy 14) from black felt.

6. Cut one of muzzle pattern piece (Easy 15) from beige felt.

7. Cut one of mane pattern piece (Easy 22) from dark brown felt.

8. Stitch or glue the body pieces together, leaving bottom open.

9. Glue eyes and pupils into place.

10. Glue muzzle into place.

11. Glue nostrils into place.

12. With fabric paint or marker, draw mouth.

13. Glue mane into place.

Optional: Cut out a tail from dark brown felt and glue to back of horse.

Easy Shark Puppet

Pattern Pieces Needed

Easy 8, 9, 34, and 35

Fabric

Felt (gray, white, black)

Other Materials Needed

White rickrack lace

Instructions

1. Enlarge, copy, and cut out all required paper pattern pieces. Tape shark (Easy 34) to shark fin (Easy 35) along dotted line to create the body.

2. Cut two of the body pattern piece (Easy 34 and 35) from gray felt.

3. Cut two of eye pattern piece (Easy 8) from white felt.

4. Cut two of pupil pattern piece (Easy 9) from black felt.

5. Stitch or glue the body pieces together, leaving bottom open.

6. Glue eyes and pupils into place.

7. Glue a row of rickrack for teeth.

Easy Wolf Puppet

Pattern Pieces Needed

Easy 1, 2, 5, 8, 9, 12, 15, and 16

Fabric

Felt (gray, white, black)

Other Materials Needed

Black fabric paint or marker

Instructions

1. Enlarge, copy, and cut out all required paper pattern pieces. Cut two of pattern piece Easy 5. Tape upper body (Easy 1) to lower body (Easy 2) along dotted line. Tape ears (Easy 5) in place. This is the body. *Note: One ear is turned backwards.*

2. Cut two of the body pattern piece (Easy 1, 2, and 5) from gray felt.

3. Cut two of eye pattern piece (Easy 8) from white felt.

4. Cut two of pupil pattern piece (Easy 9) from black felt.

5. Cut one of nose pattern piece (Easy 12) from black felt.

6. Cut one of muzzle pattern piece (Easy 15) from gray felt.

7. Cut two of fang pattern piece (Easy 16) from white felt.

8. Stitch or glue the body pieces together, leaving bottom open.

9. Glue eyes and pupils into place.

10. Glue muzzle into place.

11. Glue nose into place.

12. With fabric paint or marker, draw mouth for wolf.

13. Glue fangs into place.

Easy Fish Puppet

Pattern Pieces Needed

Easy 8, 9, and 36

Fabric

Felt (white, black, three different pastel colors for the three fish)

Other Materials Needed

Pastel fabric paint or markers (optional)

Instructions

1. Enlarge, copy, and cut out all required paper pattern pieces.

2. Cut two of eye pattern piece (Easy 8) from white felt.

3. Cut two of pupil pattern piece (Easy 9) from black felt.

4. Cut two of fish pattern piece (Easy 36) from pastel felt.

5. Stitch or glue fish pieces together, leaving bottom open.

6. Glue eyes and pupils into place.

Optional: Draw fin markings and mouth with fabric paint or markers.

Easy Turtle Puppet

Pattern Pieces Needed

Easy 8, 9, 37, and 38

Fabric

Felt (green, dark green, white, black)

Other Materials Needed

Green fabric paint or marker (optional)

Instructions

1. Enlarge, copy, and cut out all required paper pattern pieces.

2. Cut two of eye pattern piece (Easy 8) from white felt.

3. Cut two of pupil pattern piece (Easy 9) from black felt.

4. Cut two of turtle pattern piece (Easy 37) from green felt.

5. Cut one of shell pattern piece (Easy 38) from dark green felt.

6. Stitch or glue turtle pieces together, leaving bottom between legs open.

7. Glue shell into place.

8. Glue eyes and pupils into place.

Optional: With fabric paint or marker, draw a pattern on the shell.

Easy Octopus Puppet

Pattern Pieces Needed

Easy 8, 9, 39, and 40

Fabric

Felt (green, white, black)

Other Materials Needed

Black fabric paint or marker

Instructions

1. Enlarge, copy, and cut out all required paper pattern pieces. Cut eight of pattern piece Easy 40. Tape tentacles (Easy 40) to octopus (Easy 39) along dotted lines to create the body. *Note: Four of the tentacles are turned backwards.*

2. Cut two of the body pattern piece (Easy 39 and 40) from green felt.

3. Cut two of eye pattern piece (Easy 8) from white felt.

4. Cut two of pupil pattern piece (Easy 9) from black felt.

5. Stitch or glue the body pattern pieces together, leaving top open.

6. Glue eyes and pupils into place.

7. With fabric paint or marker, draw mouth for octopus.

Easy Snake Puppet

Pattern Pieces Needed

Easy 8, 9, 41, 42, 43, 44, 45, and 46

Fabric

Felt (green, white, black, red, yellow)

Other Materials Needed

Black fabric paint or marker

Instructions

1. Enlarge, copy, and cut out all required paper pattern pieces. Tape the snake's upper body (Easy 46) to the lower body (Easy 41) along dotted line. This is the body.

2. Cut two of joined pattern piece (Easy 41 and 46) from green felt.

3. Cut two of eye pattern piece (Easy 8) from white felt.

4. Cut two of pupil pattern piece (Easy 9) from black felt.

5. Cut two of fang pattern piece (Easy 42) from white felt.

6. Cut several diamond pattern pieces (Easy 43) from yellow felt.

7. Cut one of mouth pattern piece (Easy 44) from black felt.

8. Cut one of tongue pattern piece (Easy 45) from red felt.

9. Stitch or glue the body pattern pieces together, leaving bottom open.

10. Glue eyes and pupils into place.

11. Glue mouth into place.

12. Glue tongue into place.

13. Glue fangs into place.

14. Draw nostrils with fabric paint or markers.

15. Glue diamond pattern pieces on snake.

Easy Banana Puppet

Pattern Pieces Needed

Easy 8, 9, 47, and 48

Fabric

Felt (pale yellow or cream, dark yellow, white, black)

Other Materials Needed

Black fabric paint or marker

Instructions

1. Enlarge, copy, and cut out all required paper pattern pieces.

2. Cut two of eye pattern piece (Easy 8) from white felt.

3. Cut two of pupil pattern piece (Easy 9) from black felt.

4. Cut two of banana pattern piece (Easy 47) from pale yellow or cream felt.

5. Cut four of peel pattern piece (Easy 48) from dark yellow felt.

6. Stitch or glue banana pieces together, leaving bottom open.

7. Glue eyes and pupils into place.

8. With fabric paint or marker, draw mouth for banana.

9. Glue peels around base of banana, leaving upper third unglued and folded down.

Easy Bird Puppet

Pattern Pieces Needed

Easy 8, 9, 49, 50, and 51

Fabric

Felt (bright colors for "Jungle Jack" bird, green for "Little Green O'Glenn," white, black, yellow)

Other Materials Needed

Black fabric paint or marker

Instructions

1. Enlarge, copy, and cut out all required paper pattern pieces. Cut two of Easy 50. Tape wings (Easy 50) in place on Easy 49. This is the body. *Note: One wing is turned backwards.*

2. Cut two of the body pattern piece (Easy 49 and 50) from colored felt.

3. Cut two of eye pattern piece (Easy 8) from white felt.

4. Cut two of pupil pattern piece (Easy 9) from black felt.

5. Cut one of beak pattern piece (Easy 51) from yellow felt.

6. Stitch or glue the body pattern pieces together, leaving bottom open.

7. Glue eyes and pupils into place.

8. Glue beak into place.

9. Draw nostrils on beak with fabric paint or marker.

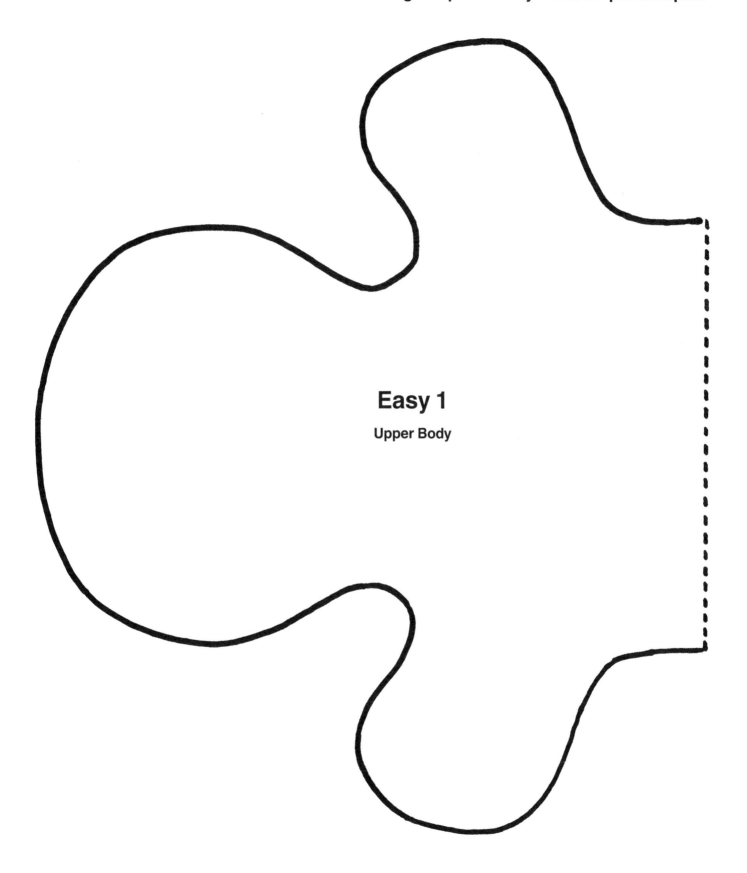

Easy 1

Upper Body

Enlarge all patterns by 110% on photocopier.

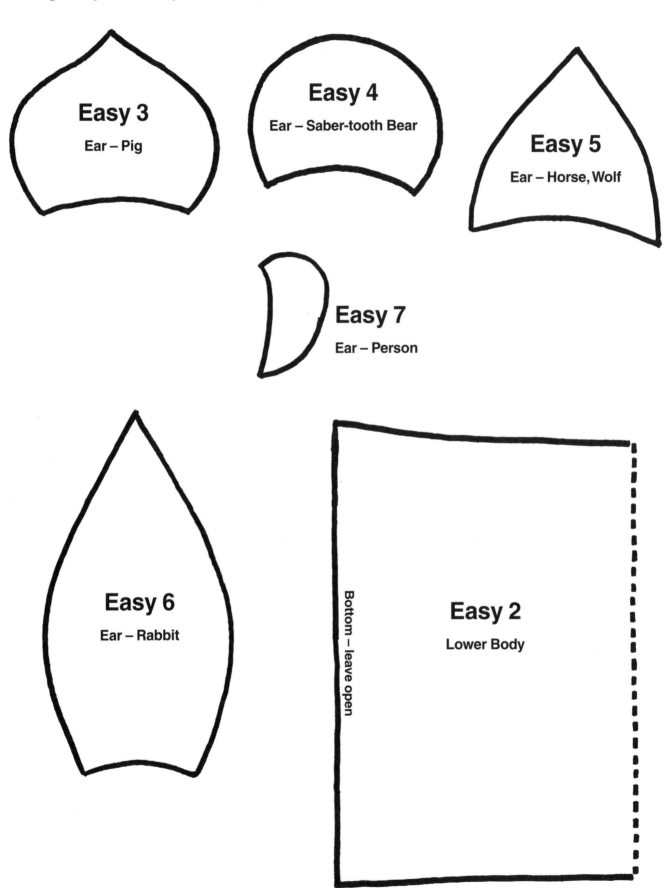

Easy 3
Ear – Pig

Easy 4
Ear – Saber-tooth Bear

Easy 5
Ear – Horse, Wolf

Easy 7
Ear – Person

Easy 6
Ear – Rabbit

Bottom – leave open

Easy 2
Lower Body

Enlarge all patterns by 110% on photocopier.

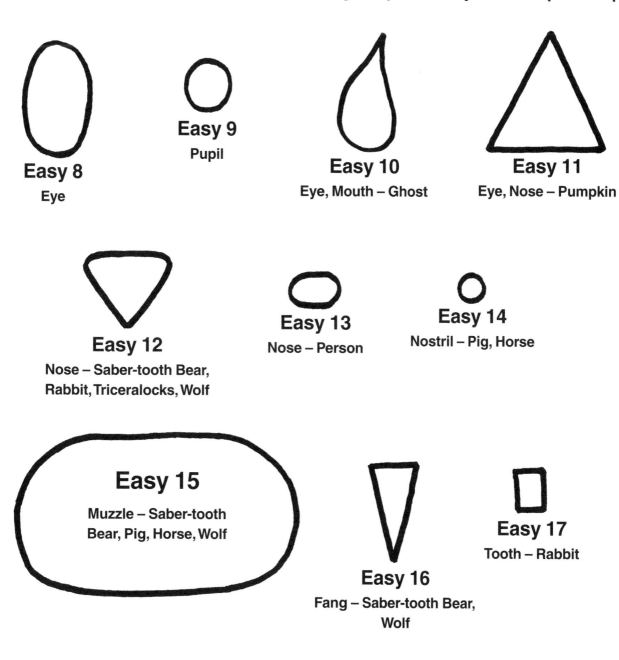

Easy 8
Eye

Easy 9
Pupil

Easy 10
Eye, Mouth – Ghost

Easy 11
Eye, Nose – Pumpkin

Easy 12
Nose – Saber-tooth Bear,
Rabbit, Triceralocks, Wolf

Easy 13
Nose – Person

Easy 14
Nostril – Pig, Horse

Easy 15
Muzzle – Saber-tooth
Bear, Pig, Horse, Wolf

Easy 16
Fang – Saber-tooth Bear,
Wolf

Easy 17
Tooth – Rabbit

Easy 18
Mouth – Pumpkin

Easy 19
Stem – Pumpkin

Enlarge all patterns by 110% on photocopier.

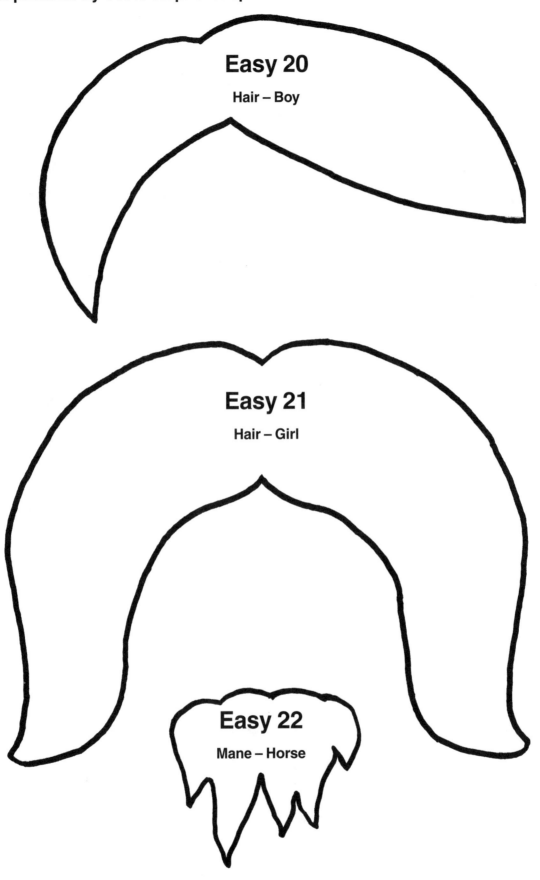

Easy 20

Hair – Boy

Easy 21

Hair – Girl

Easy 22

Mane – Horse

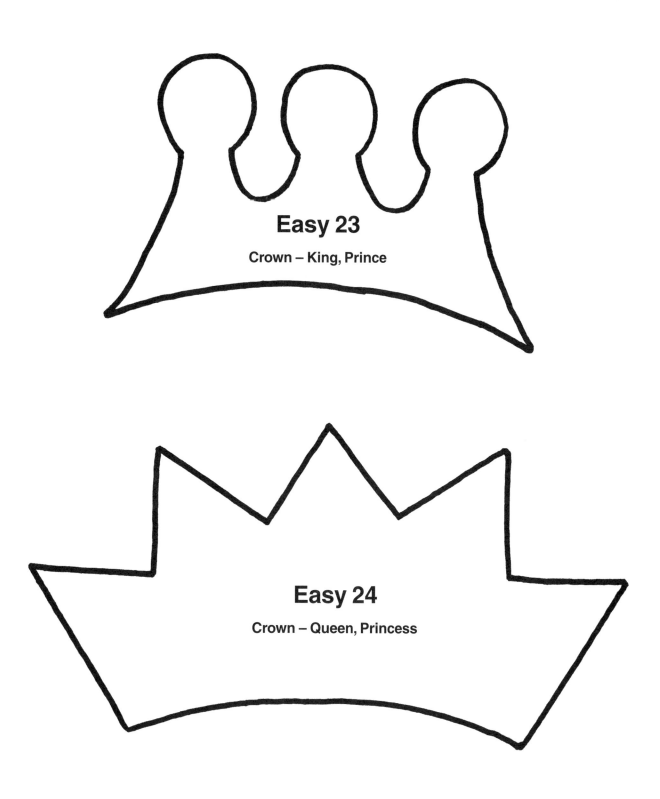

Easy 23

Crown – King, Prince

Easy 24

Crown – Queen, Princess

Enlarge all patterns by 110% on photocopier.

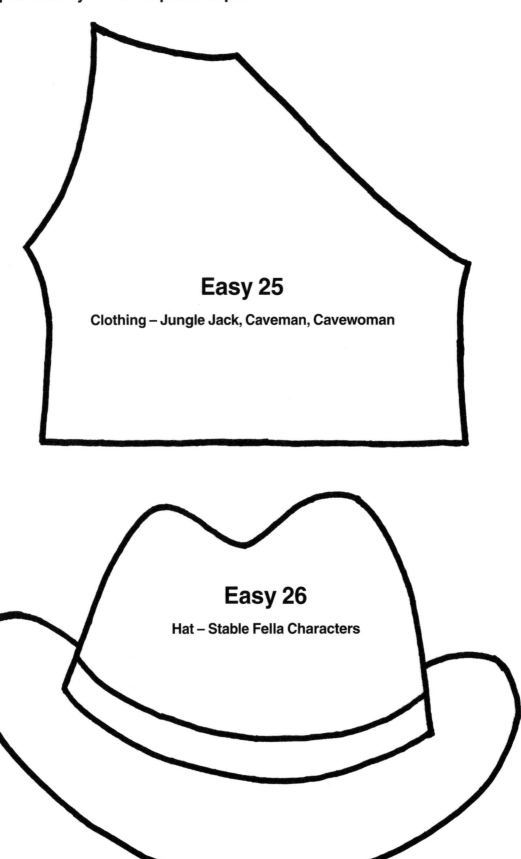

Easy 25

Clothing – Jungle Jack, Caveman, Cavewoman

Easy 26

Hat – Stable Fella Characters

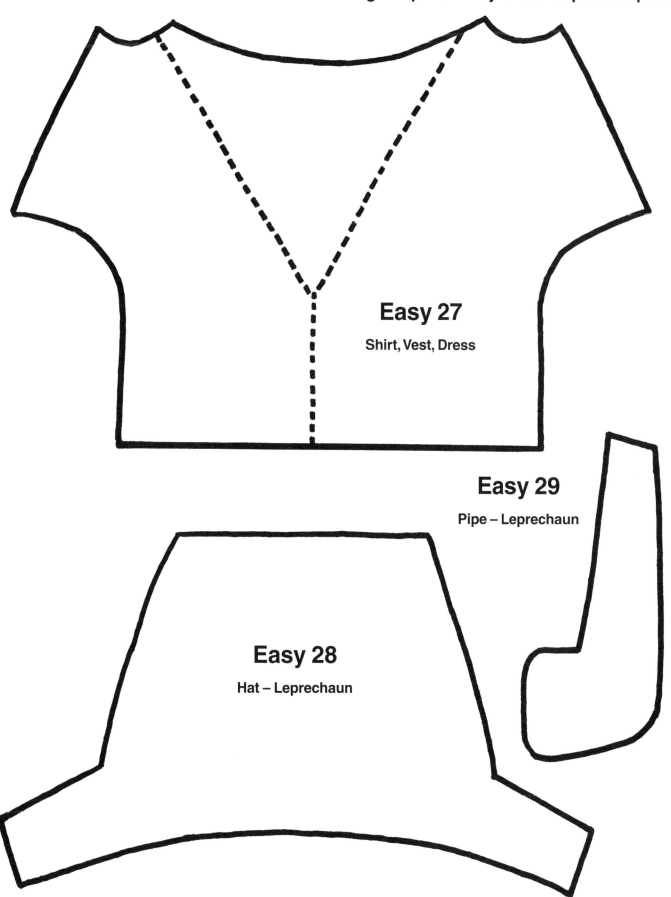

Enlarge all patterns by 110% on photocopier.

Easy 27
Shirt, Vest, Dress

Easy 29
Pipe – Leprechaun

Easy 28
Hat – Leprechaun

Enlarge all patterns by 110% on photocopier.

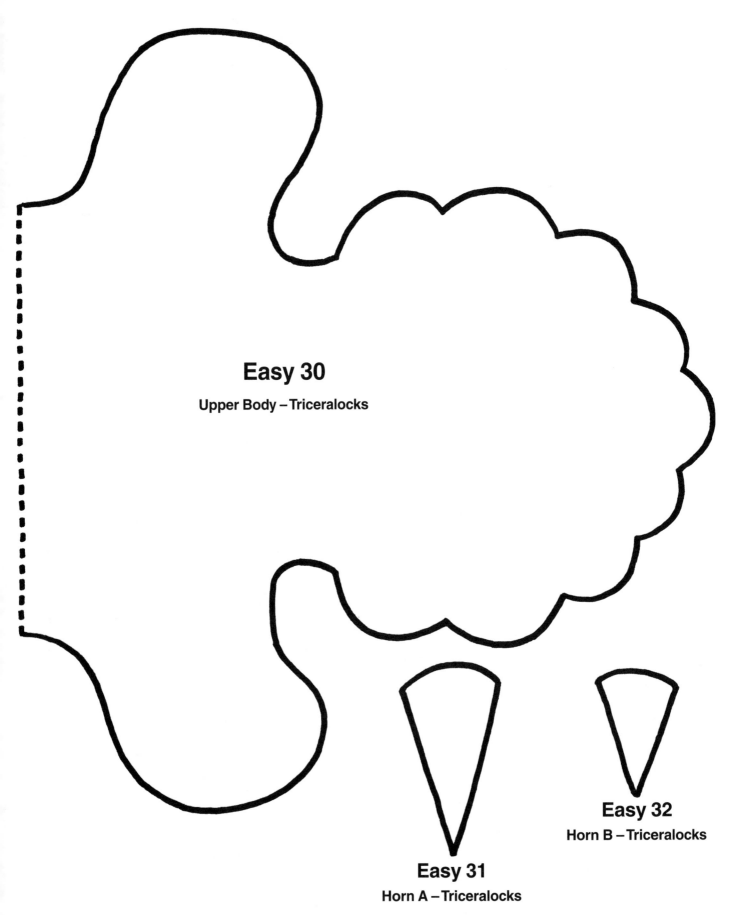

Easy 30

Upper Body – Triceralocks

Easy 32

Horn B – Triceralocks

Easy 31

Horn A – Triceralocks

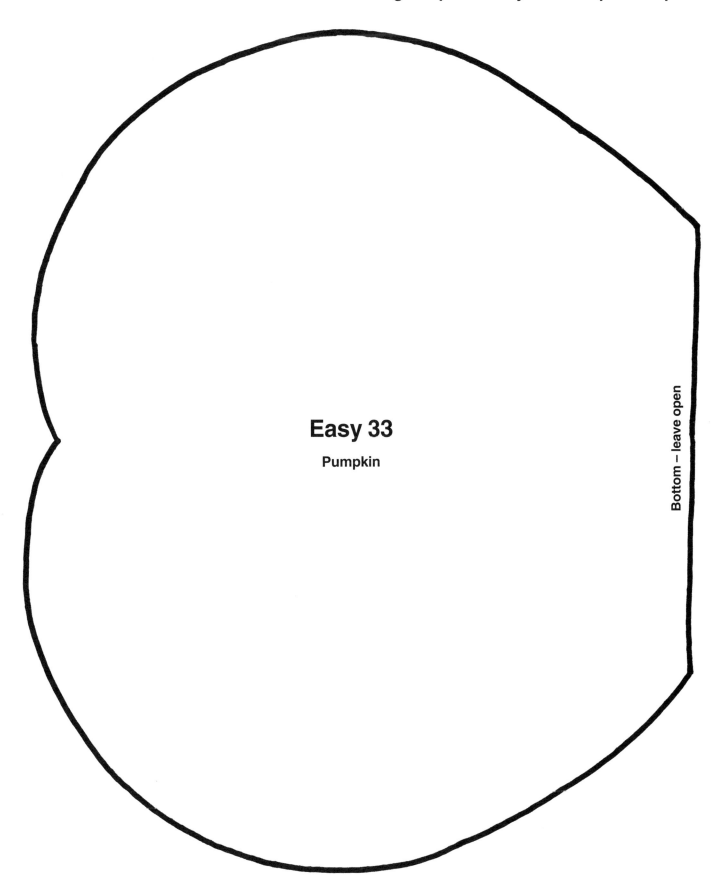

Easy 33

Pumpkin

Bottom – leave open

Enlarge all patterns by 110% on photocopier.

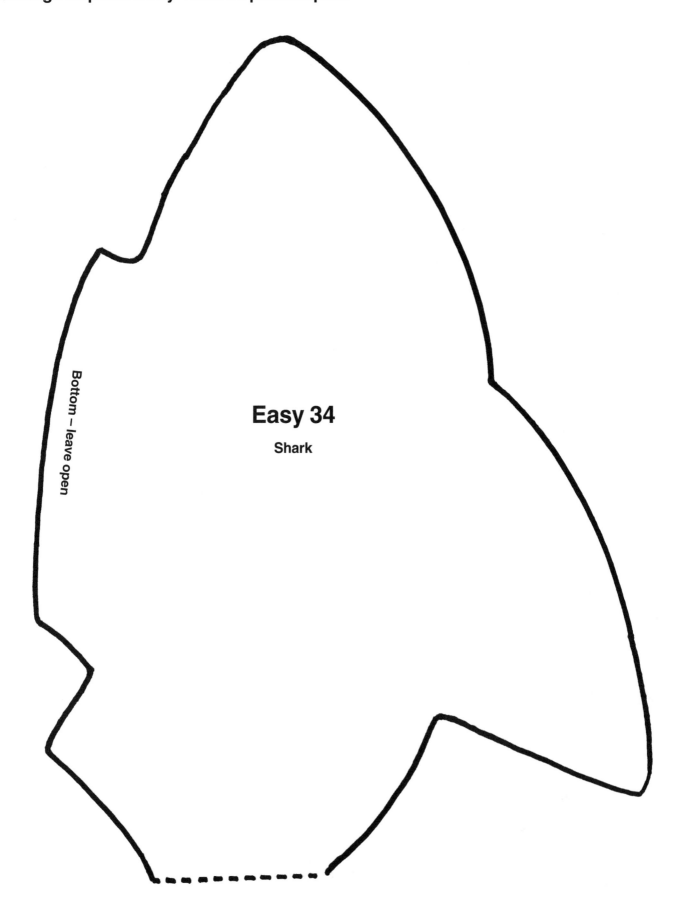

Bottom – leave open

Easy 34

Shark

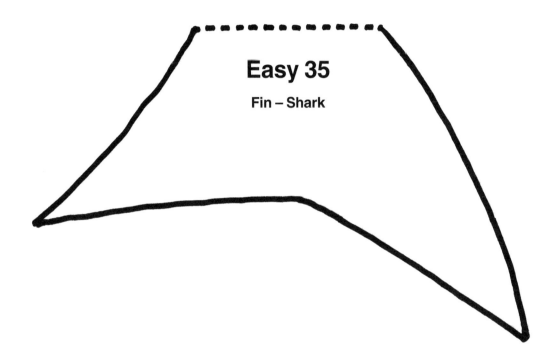

Easy 35

Fin – Shark

Enlarge all patterns by 110% on photocopier.

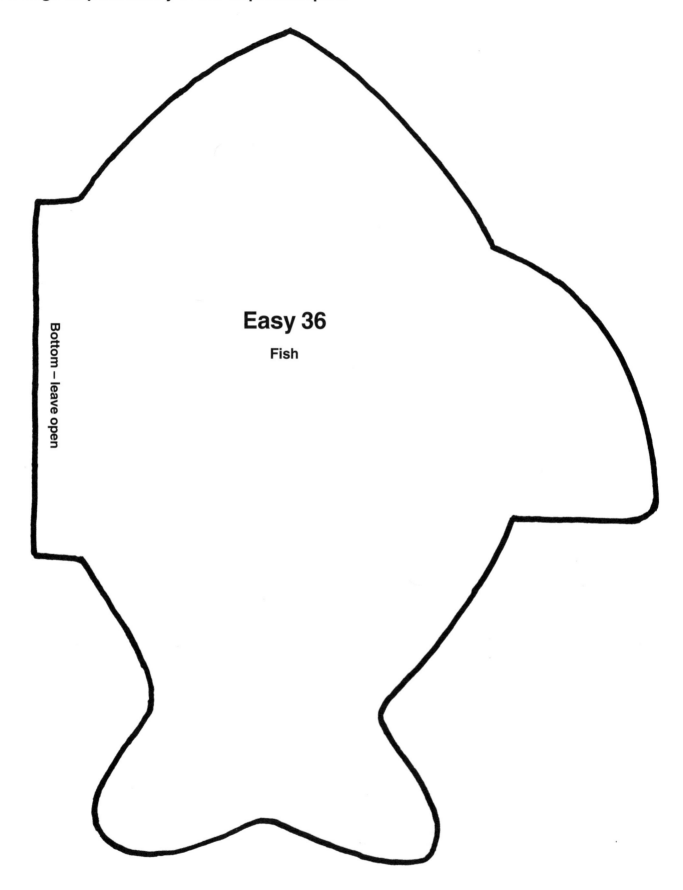

Bottom – leave open

Easy 36

Fish

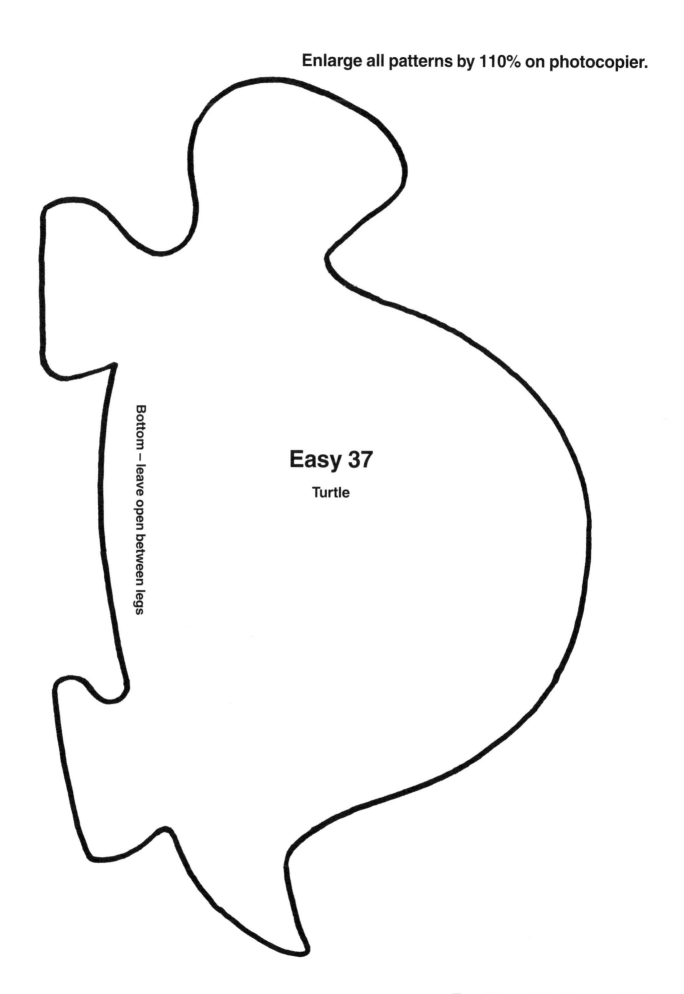

Bottom – leave open between legs

Easy 37

Turtle

Enlarge all patterns by 110% on photocopier.

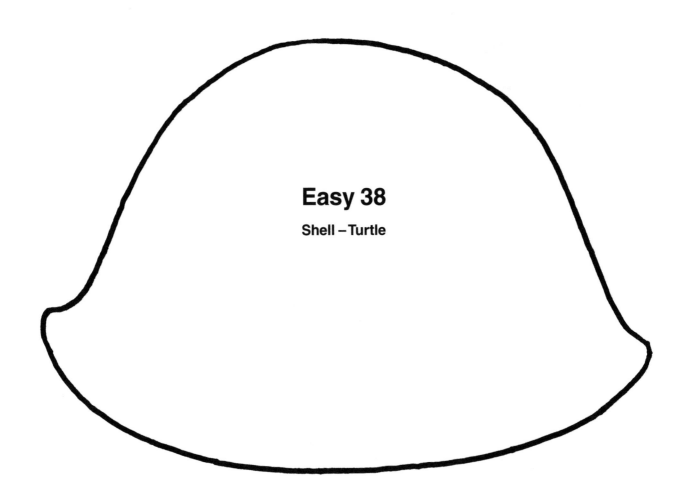

Easy 38

Shell – Turtle

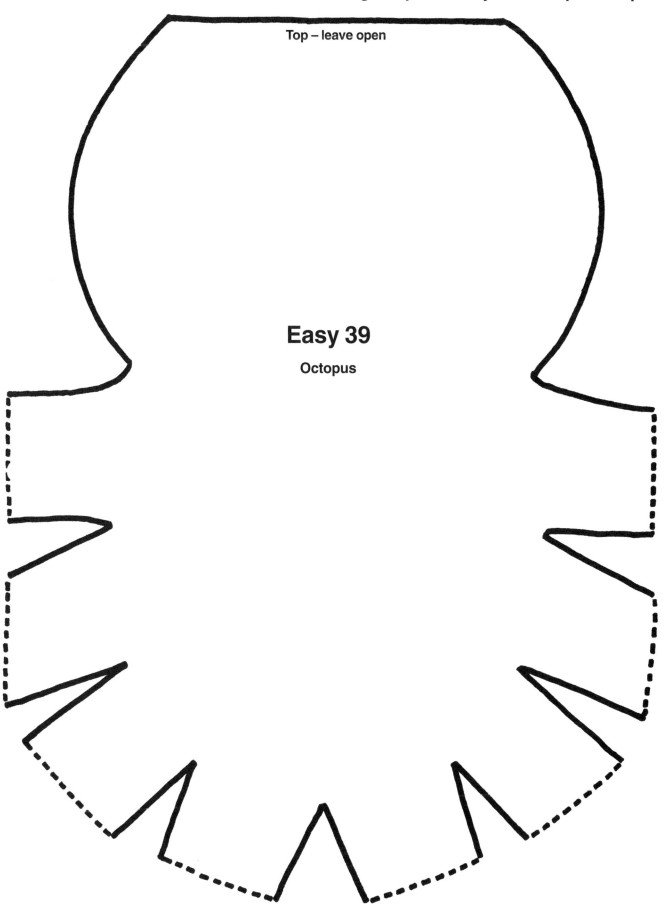

Enlarge all patterns by 110% on photocopier.

Top – leave open

Easy 39

Octopus

Enlarge all patterns by 110% on photocopier.

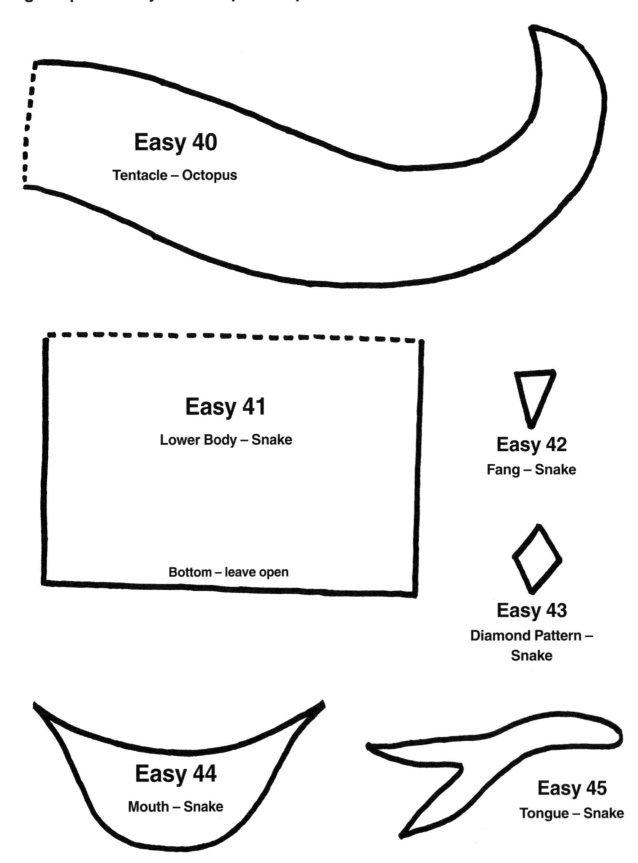

Easy 40

Tentacle – Octopus

Easy 41

Lower Body – Snake

Bottom – leave open

Easy 42

Fang – Snake

Easy 43

**Diamond Pattern –
Snake**

Easy 44

Mouth – Snake

Easy 45

Tongue – Snake

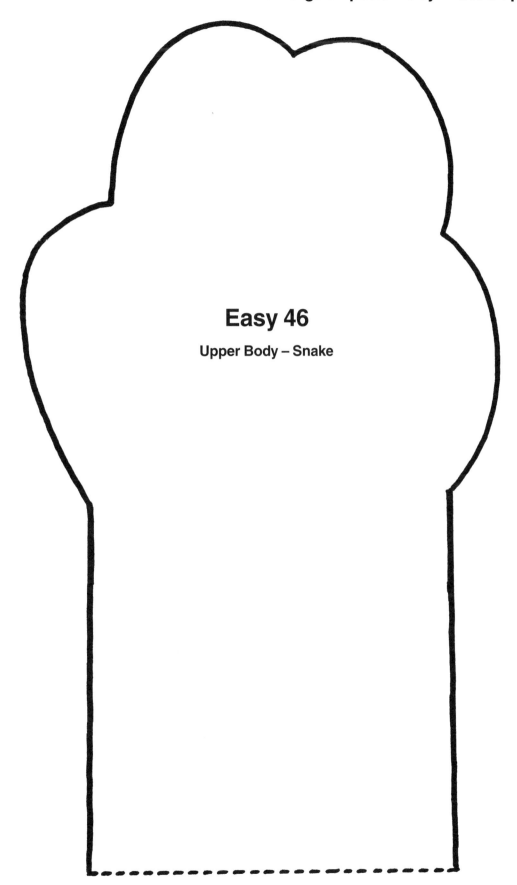

Easy 46

Upper Body – Snake

Enlarge all patterns by 110% on photocopier.

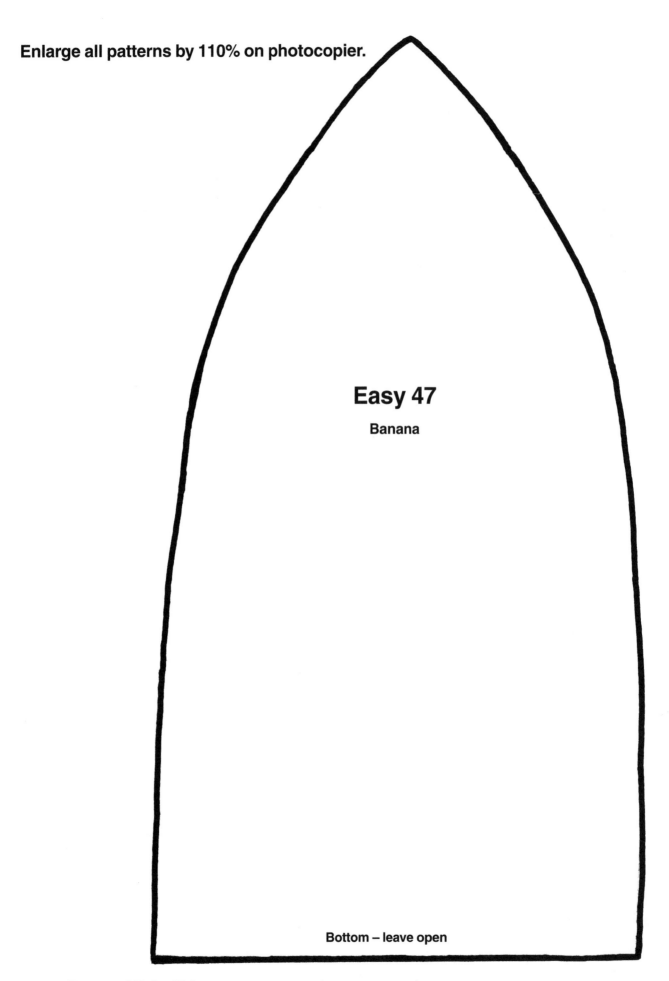

Easy 47

Banana

Bottom – leave open

Enlarge all patterns by 110% on photocopier.

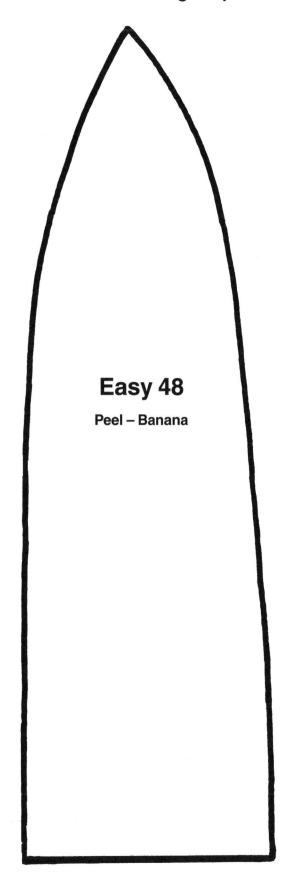

Easy 48

Peel – Banana

Enlarge all patterns by 110% on photocopier.

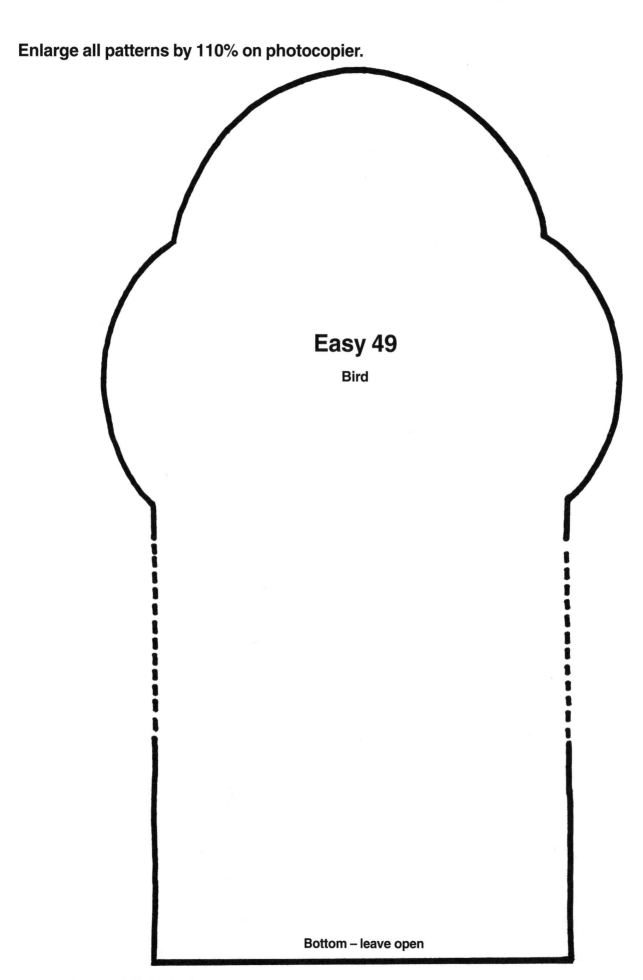

Easy 49

Bird

Bottom – leave open

Enlarge all patterns by 110% on photocopier.

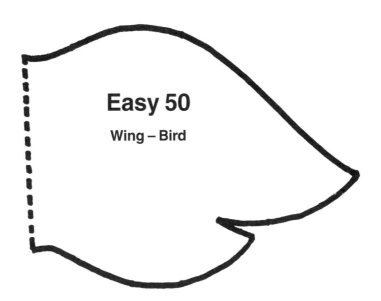

Easy 50

Wing – Bird

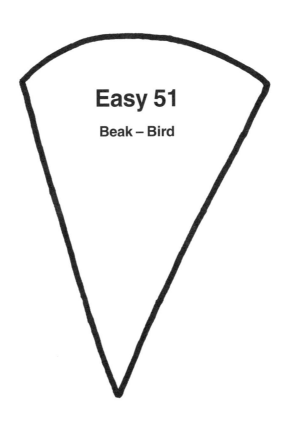

Easy 51

Beak – Bird

Making Advanced Puppets

Advanced Person Hand Puppet

Pattern Pieces Needed

Advanced 1, 2, 3, and 4

Fabric

Cotton (flesh-colored)

Other Materials Needed

Polyester stuffing, yarn for hair, colored fabric for clothing, fabric paint for facial features

Instructions

1. Enlarge, copy, and cut out all required paper pattern pieces. Tape hand (2) to body (1) matching A's. This is the body.

2. Cut two of the body pattern piece, placing straight side of pattern on fold of fabric for each.

3. Cut two of pattern piece 3 from fabric.

4. Cut one of pattern piece 4 from fabric.

5. Stitch together fabric pieces 3 from D to C.

6. With right sides together, stitch fabric piece 3 to fabric piece 4 from E to C to E. Turn piece so that right sides are facing out.

7. With right sides together, stitch joined fabric piece 1 and 2 together from B to F on both sides.

8. Push head inside body, matching neck seams. Stitch head to body at neck. Turn so that right sides of head and body are facing out.

9. Lightly stuff hands with polyester stuffing. Stitch fingers as indicated by pattern.

10. Stuff head. Attach hair and paint facial features.

11. Use suitable fabric to drape around puppet for clothing, or dress puppet in doll clothes.

Variation

Leprechaun Puppet: Use green cotton instead of flesh-colored. Follow previous directions.

Advanced Rabbit Hand Puppet

Pattern Pieces Needed

Advanced 1, 4, 5, 7, and 12

Fabric

Fun fur (brown or white), pink cotton for inside ear

Other Materials Needed

Large pom-pom for tail, small black pom-pom for nose, snap-on or roly eyes, polyester stuffing

Instructions

1. Enlarge, copy, and cut out all required paper pattern pieces. Tape paw (7) to body (1) matching A's. This is the body.

2. Cut two of the body pattern piece, placing straight side of pattern on fold of fur for each.

3. Cut two of pattern piece 5 from fur.

4. Cut one of pattern piece 4 from fur.

5. Cut two of pattern piece 12 from fur and two from pink cotton.

6. Stitch together fur pieces 5 from D to C.

7. With right sides together, stitch fur piece 5 to fur piece 4 from E to C to E. Turn piece so that right sides are facing out.

8. With right sides together, stitch the body piece 1 and 7 together from B to F on both sides.

9. Push head inside body, matching neck seams. Stitch head to body at neck. Turn so that right sides of head and body are facing out.

10. Lightly stuff paws with polyester stuffing. Stitch fingers as indicated by pattern.

11. Stuff head.

12. Stitch ears from G to H to G. Use one pink cotton piece and one fur piece for each ear. Turn pieces so right sides are facing out. Hand-stitch ears to head.

13. Fasten tail, nose, and eyes into place.

■ ▪ ■ ▪ ■ ▪ ■ ▪ ■ ▪ ■ ▪ ■ ▪ ■ ▪ ■ ▪ ■

Advanced Triceralocks Hand Puppet

Pattern Pieces Needed

Advanced 1, 4, 6, 8, 9, 10, and 11

Fabric

Fun fur (purple or orange), beige felt for horns

Other Materials Needed

Polyester stuffing, small black pom-pom for nose, snap-on or roly eyes

Instructions

1. Enlarge, copy, and cut out all required paper pattern pieces. Tape paw (10) to body (1) matching A's. This is the body.

2. Cut two of the body pattern piece, placing straight side of pattern on fold of fur for each.

3. Cut two of pattern piece 6 from fur.

4. Cut one of pattern piece 4 from fur.

5. Cut two of pattern piece 11 from fur.

6. Cut four of pattern piece 8 from beige felt.

7. Cut two of pattern piece 9 from beige felt.

8. Stitch together fur pieces 6 from D to C.

9. With right sides together, stitch fur piece 6 to fur piece 4 from E to C to E. Turn piece so that right sides are facing out.

10. With right sides together, stitch the body piece 1 and 10 together from B to F on both sides.

11. Push head inside body, matching neck seams. Stitch head to body at neck. Turn so that right sides of head and body are facing out.

12. Lightly stuff paws with polyester stuffing.

13 Stuff head.

14. With right sides together, stitch frill (11) together, leaving bottom open. Turn so that right sides are facing out. Stitch frill onto head.

15. Stitch small horns (8) together, leaving bottoms open. Turn so that right sides are facing out. Stuff with polyester stuffing. Hand-stitch horns onto head.

16. Stitch large horn (9) together, leaving bottom open. Turn so that right side is facing out. Stuff with polyester stuffing. Hand-stitch horn to head.

17. Attach pom-pom nose and eyes.

■ ▪ ■ ▪ ■ ▪ ■ ▪ ■ ▪ ■ ▪ ■ ▪ ■ ▪ ■ ▪ ■

Advanced Person Mouth Puppet

Pattern Pieces Needed

Advanced 14, 16, 18, 20, 22, and 24

Fabric

Blanket fleece or heavy cotton (flesh-colored), felt for mouth (pink)

Other Materials Needed

Polyester stuffing, yarn or fun fur for hair, snap-on or roly eyes, or fabric paint for eyes

Instructions

1. Enlarge, copy, and cut out all required paper pattern pieces. Cut two of arm (24) and turn one backwards. Tape arms (24) to body (18) matching H's. This is the body.

2. Cut four of pattern piece 14 from fabric.

3. Cut one of pattern piece 16 from fabric.

4. Cut two of the body pattern piece 18 and 24 from fabric.

5. Cut one of pattern piece 20 from pink felt.

6. Cut two of pattern piece 22 from fabric.

7. Stitch darts in fabric pieces 22.

8. With right sides together, stitch fabric pieces 22 together from J to K and from L to M.

9. Stitch mouth (20) in place, matching points J and M.

10. Turn head so that right sides are facing out.

11. With right sides together, stitch together the body piece 18 and 24 from N to O on both sides.

12. Push head inside body, matching neck seams. Stitch head to body at neck. Turn so that right sides of head and body are facing out.

13. Lightly stuff hands and arms with polyester stuffing. Stitch fingers as indicated by pattern.

14. Stuff head with polyester stuffing. Attach hair and paint facial features.

15. Stitch ears (14) together, leaving sides open. Turn so that right sides are facing out. Loosely stuff ears. Hand-stitch ears onto head.

16. Baste outer edge of nose (16). Draw in to form a ball. Loosely stuff and tie ball shut. Glue nose in place.

Variation

Troll Puppet: Use blue or green fabric. You may choose to cut larger or pointier ears for troll.

Advanced Ghost Mouth Puppet

Pattern Pieces Needed

Advanced 20 and 22

Fabric

Fleece (white), felt for mouth (black)

Other Materials Needed

Large black buttons for eyes, polyester stuffing

Instructions

1. Enlarge, copy, and cut out all required paper pattern pieces.

2. Cut one of pattern piece 20 from black felt.

3. Cut two of pattern piece 22 from fleece.

4. Stitch darts in fleece pieces 22.

5. With right sides together, stitch fleece pieces 22 together from J to K and from L to M.

6. Stitch mouth (20) in place, matching points J and M.

7. Turn head so that right sides are facing out.

8. Cut a large circle of fleece to create ghost body. In center, cut hole large enough for neck of puppet. With right sides together, stitch neck of head to hole. Turn so that right sides are facing out.

9. Stuff head with polyester stuffing.

10. Attach eyes.

Advanced Pumpkin Mouth Puppet

Pattern Pieces Needed

Advanced 20 and 22 (enlarge pattern pieces to desired size on photocopier)

Fabric

Fun fur (orange); felt for mouth, eyes, and nose (black); felt for stem (green)

Other Materials Needed

Polyester stuffing, gold cord

Instructions

1. Enlarge, copy, and cut out both required paper pattern pieces.

2. Cut one of pattern piece 20 from black felt.

3. Cut two of pattern piece 22 from fur.

4. Stitch darts in fur pieces 22.

5. With right sides together, stitch fur pieces 22 together from J to K and from L to M.

6. Stitch mouth (20) in place, matching points J and M.

7. Turn pumpkin so that right sides are facing out.

8. Stuff with polyester stuffing.

9. Using gold cord, glue lines from top to bottom of pumpkin, creating sections.

10. Cut piece of green felt for pumpkin stem. Glue to top of pumpkin.

11. Cut three triangles from black felt. Glue on for eyes and nose.

Advanced Saber-tooth Bear Mouth Puppet

Pattern Pieces Needed

Advanced 13, 15, 16, 18, 21, 23, and 24
Note: You will need to make three different sizes of bears. Use original pattern size for Baby Bear, and enlarge Ma and Pa Bear to desired sizes.

Fabric

Fun fur (leopard print), felt for mouth and inner ear (pink), felt for nose (black), felt for teeth (white)

Other Materials Needed

Polyester stuffing, snap-on or roly eyes

Instructions

1. Enlarge, copy, and cut out all required paper pattern pieces. Cut two of arm (24) and turn one backwards. Tape arms (24) to body (18) matching H's. This is the body.

2. Cut two of pattern piece 13 from fur and two from pink felt.

3. Cut four of pattern piece 15 from white felt.

4. Cut one of pattern piece 16 from black felt.

5. Cut two of the body pattern piece 18 and 24 from fur.

6. Cut one of pattern piece 21 from pink felt.

7. Cut two of pattern piece 23 from fur

8. Stitch darts in fur pieces 23.

9. With right sides together, stitch fur pieces 23 together from J to K and from L to M.

10. Stitch mouth (21) in place, matching points J and M.

11. Turn head so that right sides are facing out.

12. With right sides together, stitch together the body piece 18 and 24 from N to O on both sides.

13. Push head inside body, matching neck seams. Stitch head to body at neck.

14. Turn so that right sides of head and body are facing out.

15. Loosely stuff hands and arms with polyester stuffing. Stitch fingers as indicated on pattern.

16. Stuff head with polyester stuffing. Attach eyes.

17. Stitch ears (13) together, using one pink piece and one fur piece for each ear. Leave the bottoms open. Turn so that right sides are facing out. Hand-stitch ears onto head.

18. Baste outer edge of nose (16). Draw in to form a ball. Lightly stuff and tie ball shut. Glue nose in place.

19. Stitch fangs together, leaving top open. Turn so that right sides are facing out. Stuff fangs and glue into place.

Advanced Pig Mouth Puppet

Pattern Pieces Needed

Advanced 17, 18, 21, 23, 24, and 26

Fabric

Fun fur (pink); felt for mouth, inner ear, and nostrils (dark pink); felt for hoof (brown)

Other Materials Needed

Polyester stuffing, snap-on or roly eyes, pink pipe cleaner for tail (optional)

Instructions

1. Enlarge, copy, and cut out all required paper pattern pieces. Cut two of arm (24) and turn one backwards. Tape arms (24) to body (18) matching H's. This is the body.

2. Cut hands off at line I.

3. Cut two of pattern piece 17 from fur and two from pink felt.

4. Cut two of the body pattern piece 18 and 24 from fabric.

5. Cut one of pattern piece 21 from pink felt.

6. Cut two of pattern piece 23 from fur.

7. Cut four of pattern piece 26 from brown felt.

8. Stitch darts in fur pieces 23.

9. With right sides together, stitch fur pieces 23 together from J to K and from L to M.

10. Stitch mouth (21) in place, matching points J and M.

11. Turn head so that right sides are facing out.

12. Stitch one hoof (26) to each arm, matching I's.

13. With right sides together, stitch together the body piece 18, 24, and 26 from N to O on both sides.

14. Push head inside body, matching neck seams. Stitch head to body at neck. Turn so that right sides of head and body are facing out.

15. Loosely stuff hooves and arms with polyester stuffing.

16. Stuff head with polyester stuffing. Attach eyes.

17. Cut two small circles from pink felt for nostrils. Glue in place.

18. Stitch ears (17) together, using one pink piece and one fur piece for each ear. Leave the bottoms open. Turn so that right sides are facing out. Hand-stitch ears onto head.

19. Glue tail to back (optional).

Advanced Horse Mouth Puppet

Pattern Pieces Needed

Advanced 18, 19, 21, 23, 24 and 25

Fabric

Fun fur (light brown); felt for mouth, inner ear and nostrils (pink); felt for hooves (black)
Note: Horse in "Stable Fella" is white.

Other Materials Needed

Polyester stuffing, snap-on or roly eyes, dark-brown yarn for mane and tail

Instructions

1. Enlarge, copy, and cut out all required paper pattern pieces. Cut two of arm (24) and turn one backwards. Tape arms (24) to body (18) matching H's. This is the body.

2. Cut hands off at line I.

3. Cut two of pattern piece 19 from fur and two from pink felt.

4. Cut two of the body pattern piece 18 and 24 from fur.

5. Cut one of pattern piece 21 from pink felt.

6. Cut two of pattern piece 23 from fur.

7. Cut four of pattern piece 25 from black felt.

8. Stitch darts in fur pieces 23.

9. With right sides together, stitch fur pieces 23 together from J to K and from L to M.

10. Stitch mouth (21) in place, matching points J and M.

11. Turn head so that right sides are facing out.

12. Stitch one hoof (25) to each arm, matching I's.

13. With right sides together, stitch together the body piece 18, 25, and 26 from N to O on both sides.

14. Push head inside body, matching neck seams. Stitch head to body at neck. Turn so that right sides of head and body are facing out.

15. Loosely stuff hooves and arms with polyester stuffing.

16. Stuff head with polyester stuffing. Attach eyes.

17. Cut two small circles from pink felt for nostrils. Glue in place.

18 Stitch ears (19) together, using one pink piece and one fur piece for each ear. Leave the bottoms open. Turn so that right sides are facing out. Hand-stitch ears onto head.

19. Make horse's mane by tying pieces of yarn together. Glue yarn onto top of head and neck.

20. Make horse's tail by tying long pieces of yarn together. Glue tail to back of body (optional).

Advanced Shark Mouth Puppet

Pattern Pieces Needed

Advanced 27, 28, 29, 32, and 33

Fabric

Blanket fleece or canvas cotton (gray), felt for mouth (pink)

Other Materials Needed

Polyester stuffing, snap-on or roly eyes, white rickrack for teeth

Instructions

1. Enlarge, copy, and cut out all required paper pattern pieces. Tape pattern piece 33 on side of pattern piece 27, matching E's, and tape pattern piece 32 on other side of pattern piece 27, matching F's. This is the shark's body.

2. Cut two of the body pattern piece 27, 32, and 33 from fabric.

3. Cut two of pattern piece 28 from fabric.

4. Cut one of pattern piece 29 from pink felt.

5. Stitch darts in fabric pieces 28.

6. With right sides together, stitch pattern pieces 28 together from A to B and from C to D.

7. Stitch mouth (29) in place, matching points A and D.

8. Turn head so that right sides are facing out.

9. With right sides together, stitch sides of body together. Leave both ends open.

10. Push head inside body, matching neck seams. Stitch head to body at neck. Turn so that right sides of head and body are facing out.

11. Stuff head and fins.

12. Fasten eyes into place.

13. Fasten rickrack around mouth for teeth.

Advanced Wolf Mouth Puppet

Pattern Pieces Needed

Advanced 16, 27, 29, 30, 31, and 34

Fabric

Fun fur (gray), extra plush fun fur for tail (gray), felt for mouth and inside ears (pink), felt for nose (black), felt for teeth (white)

Other Materials Needed

Polyester stuffing, snap-on or roly eyes

Instructions

1. Enlarge, copy, and cut out all required paper pattern pieces.

2. Cut one of pattern piece 16 from black felt.

3. Cut two of pattern piece 27 from gray fun fur.

4. Cut one of pattern piece 29 from pink felt.

5. Cut two of pattern piece 30 from gray fun fur.

6. Cut two of pattern piece 31 from fun fur and two from pink felt.

7. Cut two of pattern piece 34 from extra plush fur.

8. Stitch darts in fur pieces 30.

9. With right sides together, stitch fur pieces 30 together from A to B and from C to D.

10. Stitch mouth (29) in place, matching points A and D.

11. Turn head so that right sides are facing out.

12. With right sides together, stitch sides of body together. Leave both ends open.

13. Push head inside body, matching neck seams. Stitch head to body at neck. Turn so that right sides of head and body are facing out.

14. Stuff head with polyester stuffing.

15. Stitch ears (31) together, using one pink piece and one fur piece for each ear. Leave the bottoms open. Turn so that the right sides are facing out. Hand-stitch ears onto head.

16. Fasten eyes into place. Cut teeth from white felt. Glue into place.

17. Stitch tail pieces together, leaving end open. Stuff tail with polyester stuffing. Hand-stitch to back of body, matching G.

Advanced Fish Hand Puppet

Note: You will need to make three fish puppets. Choose three different colors of fabric for your fish.

Pattern Pieces Needed

Advanced 35 and 36

Fabric

Blanket fleece or canvas cotton (three different colors)

Other Materials Needed

Snap-on or roly eyes

Instructions

1. Enlarge, copy, and cut out all required paper pattern pieces. Tape pattern piece 36 to pattern piece 35, matching A's. This is the body.

2. Cut two of the body pattern piece 35 and 36 from fabric.

3. Stitch entire body from C to D, leaving side B open.

4. Turn so that right sides are facing out.

5. Stitch fin and tail as indicated on pattern.

6. Fasten eyes into place.

Advanced Turtle Hand Puppet

Pattern Pieces Needed

Advanced 37, 38, and 39

Fabric

Blanket fleece or canvas cotton (green)

Other Materials Needed

Polyester stuffing, snap-on or roly eyes, fabric paint for shell (optional)

Instructions

1. Enlarge, copy, and cut out all required paper pattern pieces. Make four copies of pattern piece 39. Turn two of piece 39 backwards. Tape pieces together to form a large oval. This is the shell.

2. Cut out paper pattern pieces 37 and 38. Join the body, matching E's.

3. Cut one of shell pattern piece 39 from fabric.

4. Cut two of the body pattern piece 37 and 38 from fabric.

5. With right sides together, stitch entire body together from G to H, leaving F side open.

6. Stuff head with polyester stuffing.

7. Attach eyes into place.

8. Stitch four darts on fabric piece 39.

9. Baste around outer edge of shell. Draw fabric in to form slightly rounded shell. Stuff with polyester stuffing.

10. Hand-stitch shell onto top of body.

11. Paint pattern on shell with fabric paint (optional).

Advanced Octopus Hand Puppet

Pattern Pieces Needed

Advanced 40, 41, and 42

Fabric

Blanket fleece or fun fur (green)

Other Materials Needed

Polyester stuffing, snap-on or roly eyes

Instructions

1. Enlarge, copy, and cut out all required paper pattern pieces. Make eight copies of pattern piece 41.

2. Tape one tentacle (41) to each arm on body (40) matching I's. This is the body.
   Note: Four of the tentacles are turned backwards.

3. Cut one of pattern piece 42 from fabric.

4. Cut two of the body pattern piece 40 and 41 from fabric.

5. With right sides together, stitch entire body and tentacles from J to K, leaving L side open.

6. Turn so that right sides are facing out.
   Note: This can be a difficult piece to turn. Try using a knitting needle or stick to help turn the tentacles.

7. Stuff end of tentacles.

8. Stitch darts on head (42).

9. Baste around outer edge of head. Draw fabric in to form rounded head. Stuff with polyester stuffing.

10. Fasten eyes into place.

11. Hand-stitch head onto top center of body.

Advanced Snake Mouth Puppet

Pattern Pieces Needed

Advanced 43, 44, and 45

Fabric

Fun fur (green), felt for mouth (pink), felt for tongue (red)

Other Materials Needed

Snap-on or roly eyes

Instructions

1. Cut out all required paper pattern pieces.

2. Extend head and body pattern (43) by 14" at neck.

3. Cut two of pattern piece 43 from fur.

4. Cut one of pattern piece 44 from pink felt.

5. Cut one of pattern piece 45 from red felt.

6. With right sides together, stitch together fur pieces 43 from K to bottom of neck on both sides. Do not stitch around J. Leave bottom open.

7. Stitch mouth (44) in place, matching points J and K.

8. Turn snake so that right sides are facing out.

9. Fasten eyes into place.

10. Glue tongue into place.

Advanced Banana Mouth Puppet

Pattern Pieces Needed

Advanced 46, 47, and 48

Fabric

Fun fur (yellow) for peel, blanket fleece for banana and outer mouth (pale yellow), felt for inner mouth (beige)

Other Materials Needed

Polyester stuffing, snap-on or roly eyes, gold cord

Instructions

1. Enlarge, copy, and cut out all required paper pattern pieces.

2. Extend head and body pattern (46) by 7" at neck.

3. Extend peel pattern (48) by 7" at base.

4. Cut two of pattern piece 46 from pale yellow fleece.

5. On one of piece 46 cut out center oval as indicated on pattern.

6. Cut one of pattern piece 47 from pale yellow fleece and one from beige felt. With pale yellow fleece piece, cut out center oval as indicated on pattern.

7. Cut four of pattern piece 48 from yellow fun fur.

8. With right sides together, stitch pattern piece 46 with the center cut out to pattern piece 47 with the center cut out. Stitch around the oval opening, matching L's.

9. Push the mouth (47) through the opening. Now you will have the wrong side of the body and the right side of the mouth facing you.

10. With right sides together place the full mouth piece (47) over the attached mouth piece. Stitch around the circle, covering the opening. Push the mouth back through the opening.

11. With right sides together, stitch body pieces (46) together, leaving bottom open.

12. Turn so that right sides are facing out.

13. Stuff top of head with polyester stuffing.

14. With right sides together, stitch peel sections together from bottom to M. When all pieces are stitched together they will form a circle.

15. Turn so that right sides are facing out.

16. Insert puppet body inside ring of peels. Lightly hand-stitch into place.

17. Hand-stitch or glue gold cord up seams of each peel and all the way to the tips. The cord will resemble the sides of a banana.

18. Fasten eyes into place.

Advanced Bird Mouth Puppet

Pattern Pieces Needed

Advanced 49, 50, 51, and 52

Fabric

Fun fur (bright colors for "Jungle Jack" bird, green for "Little Green O'Glenn"), felt for beak (yellow)

Other Material Needed

Polyester stuffing, snap-on or roly eyes

Instructions

1. Enlarge, copy, and cut out all required paper pattern pieces.

2. Extend body pattern (49) by 5" at neck.

3. Cut two of pattern piece 49 from fur.

4. On one of piece 49 cut out center oval as indicated on pattern.

5. Cut two of pattern piece 50 from yellow felt.

6. On one 50 piece cut center oval out as indicated on pattern.

7. Cut four of pattern piece 51 from fur.

8. Cut two of pattern piece 52 from fur.

9. With right sides together, stitch pattern piece 49 with the center cut out to pattern piece 50 with the center cut out. Stitch around the oval opening, matching L's.

10. Push beak (50) through the opening in pattern piece 49. Now you will have the wrong side of the body and the right side of the beak facing you.

11. With right sides together, place the full beak piece over the attached beak piece. Stitch around the beak, matching N's. Leave no opening. Push the beak back through the opening.

12. With right sides together, stitch body pieces (49) together, leaving bottom open.

13. Turn so that right sides are facing out.

14. Stuff top of head with polyester stuffing.

15. With right sides together, stitch two wing sections together, leaving P side open. Make two wings.

16. Turn so that right sides are facing out.

17. Hand-stitch wings into place on bird.

18. With right sides together, stitch tail sections together, leaving O side open.

19. Turn so that right sides are facing out.

20. Hand-stitch tail into place on bird.

21. Fasten eyes into place.

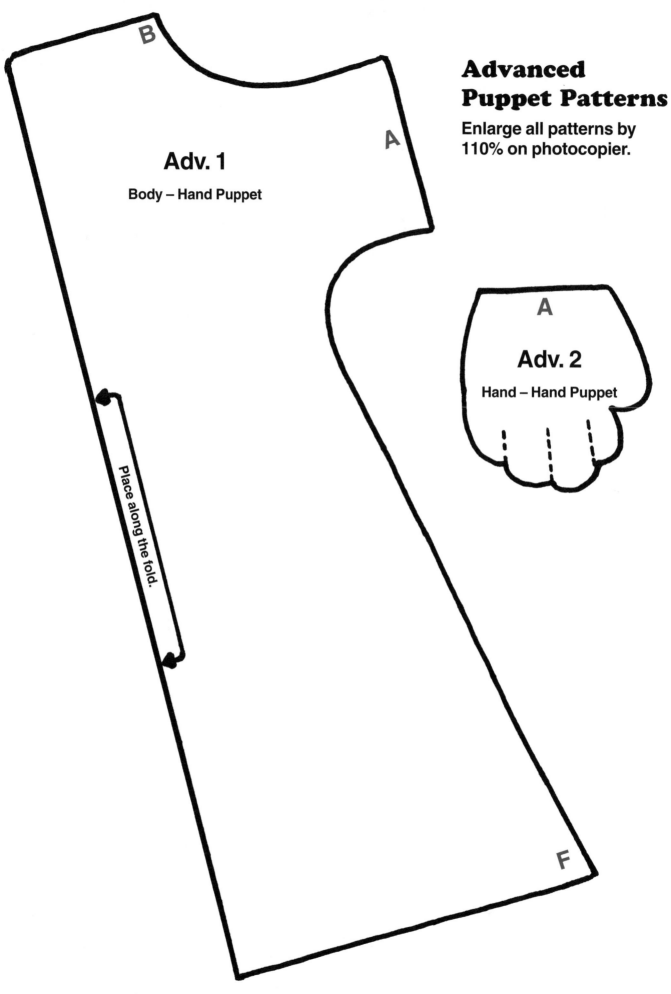

Adv. 1

Body – Hand Puppet

Place along the fold.

B

A

F

**Advanced
Puppet Patterns**

Enlarge all patterns by
110% on photocopier.

A

Adv. 2

Hand – Hand Puppet

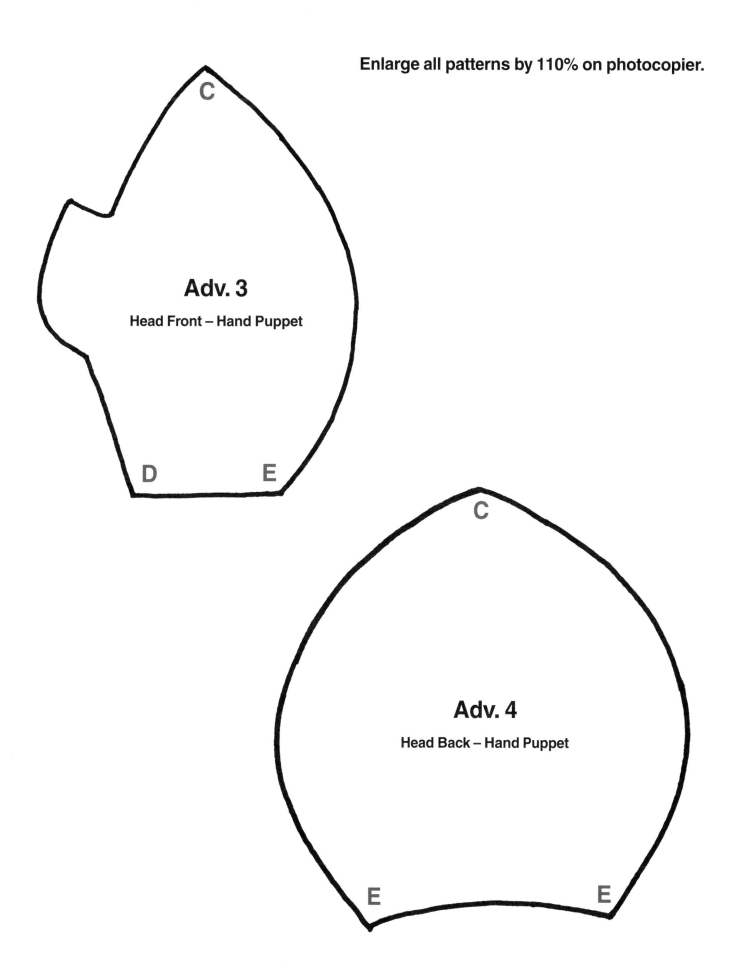

Enlarge all patterns by 110% on photocopier.

C

Adv. 3

Head Front – Hand Puppet

D   E

C

Adv. 4

Head Back – Hand Puppet

E   E

Enlarge all patterns by 110% on photocopier.

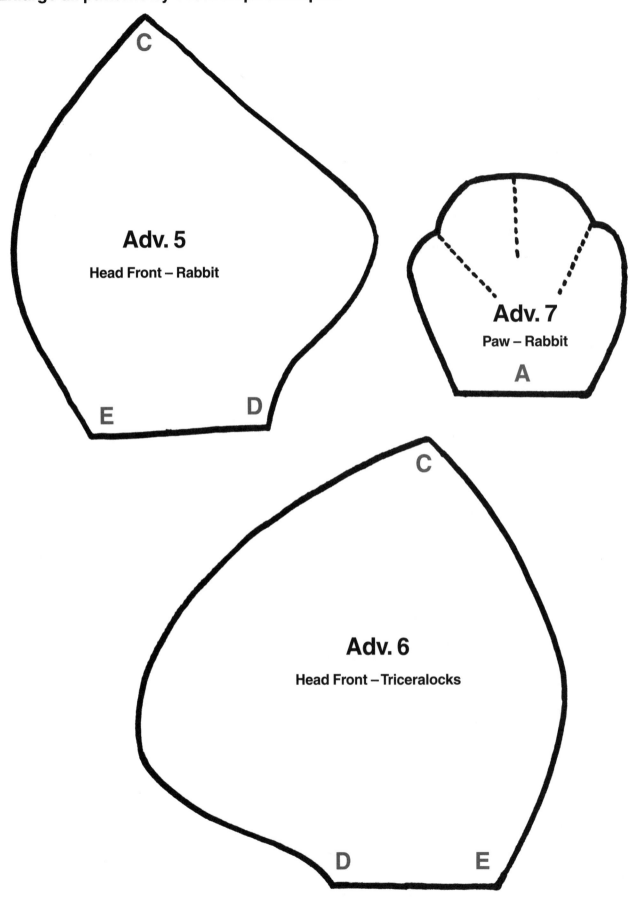

C

Adv. 5

Head Front – Rabbit

E   D

Adv. 7

Paw – Rabbit

A

C

Adv. 6

Head Front – Triceralocks

D   E

Enlarge all patterns by 110% on photocopier.

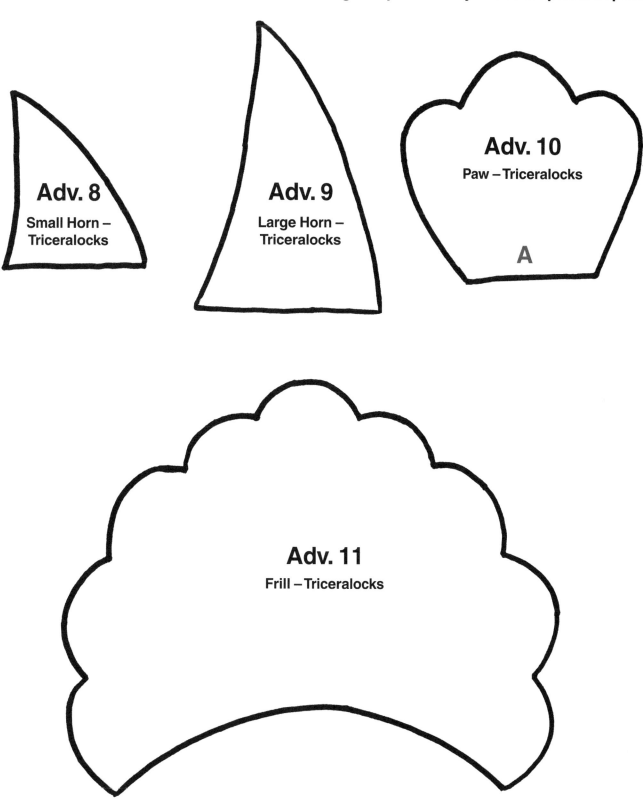

Adv. 8
Small Horn –
Triceralocks

Adv. 9
Large Horn –
Triceralocks

Adv. 10
Paw – Triceralocks

A

Adv. 11
Frill – Triceralocks

Enlarge all patterns by 110% on photocopier.

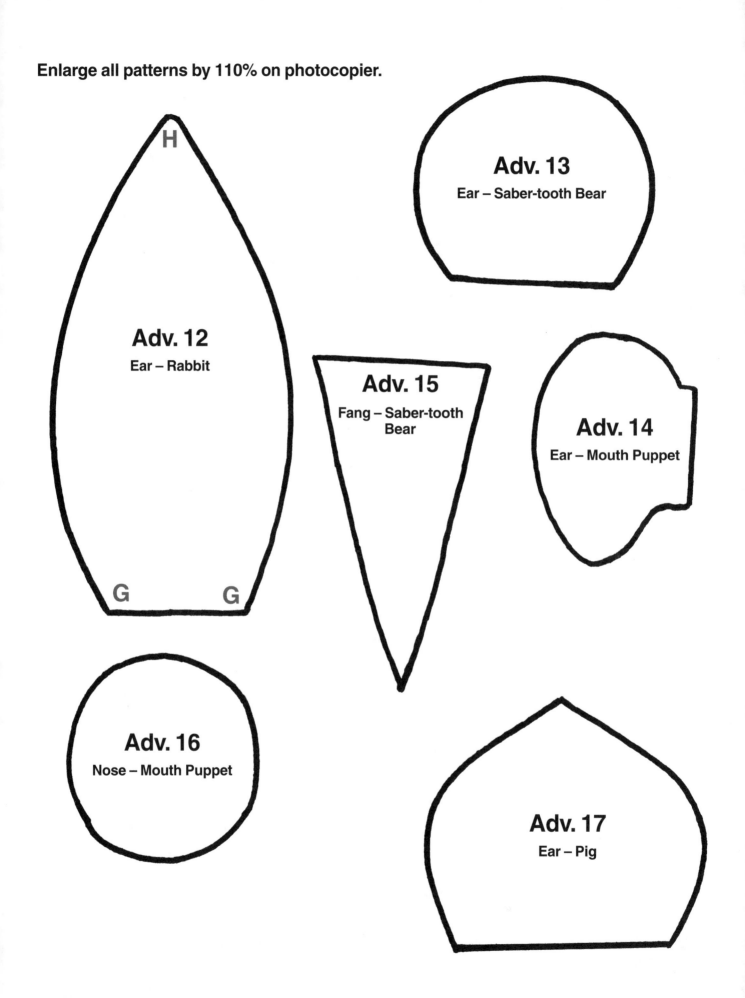

H

Adv. 12

Ear – Rabbit

G   G

Adv. 13

Ear – Saber-tooth Bear

Adv. 15

Fang – Saber-tooth
Bear

Adv. 14

Ear – Mouth Puppet

Adv. 16

Nose – Mouth Puppet

Adv. 17

Ear – Pig

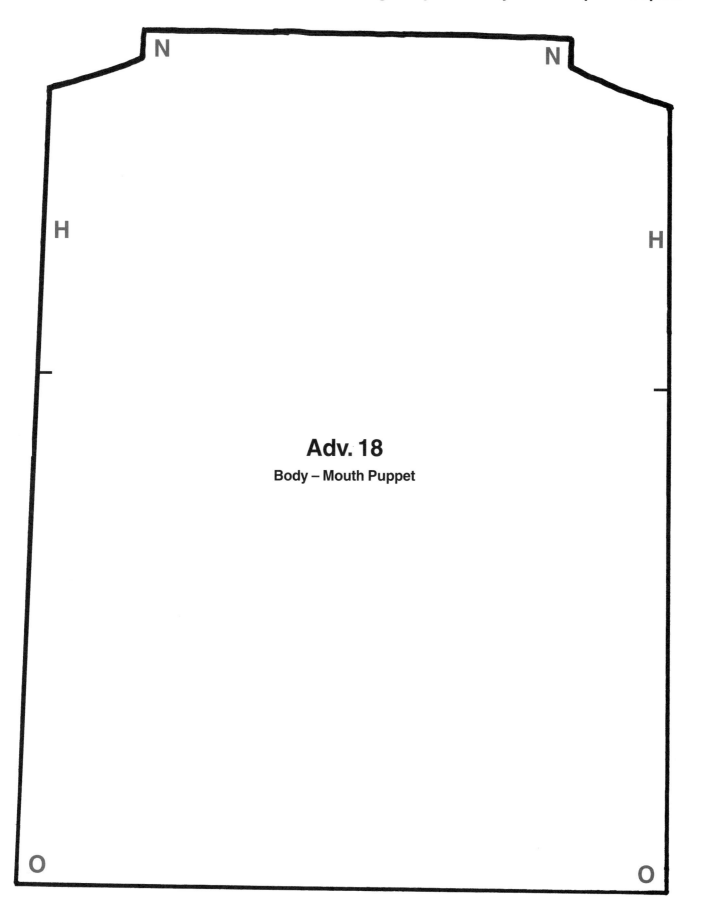

Adv. 18

Body – Mouth Puppet

Enlarge all patterns by 110% on photocopier.

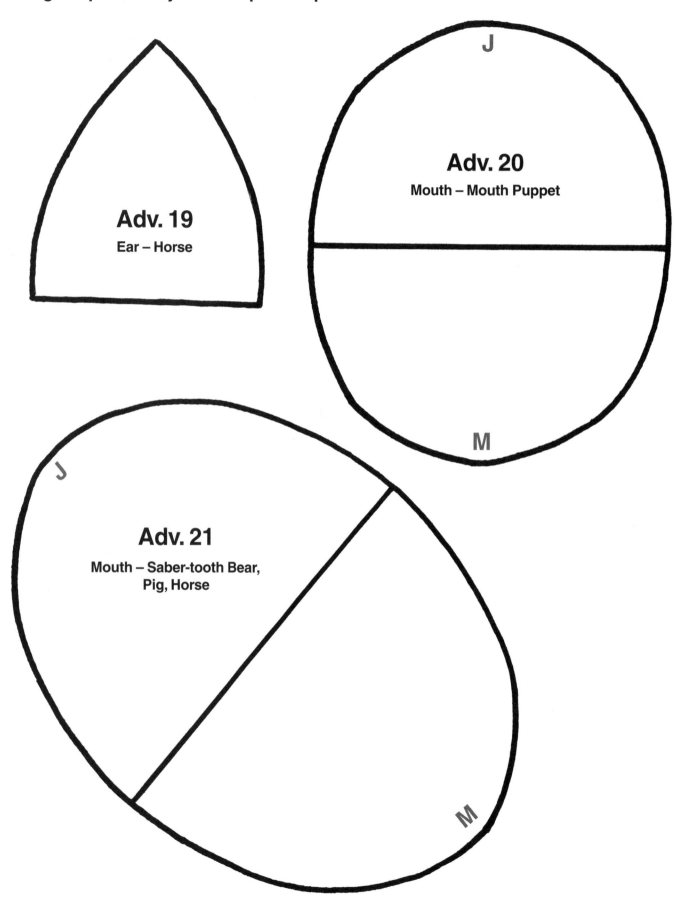

Adv. 19

Ear – Horse

Adv. 20

Mouth – Mouth Puppet

J

M

Adv. 21

Mouth – Saber-tooth Bear,
Pig, Horse

J

M

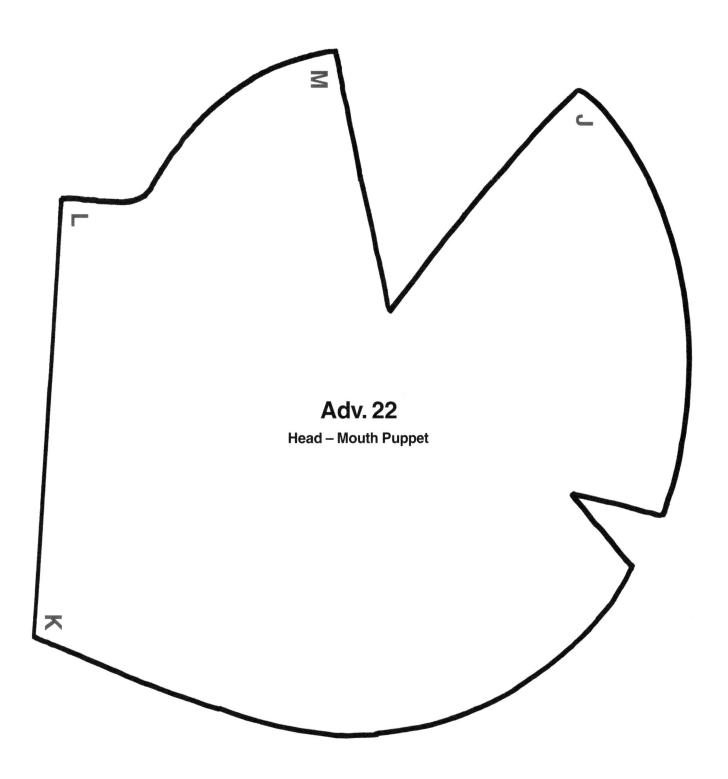

Adv. 22

Head – Mouth Puppet

Enlarge all patterns by 110% on photocopier.

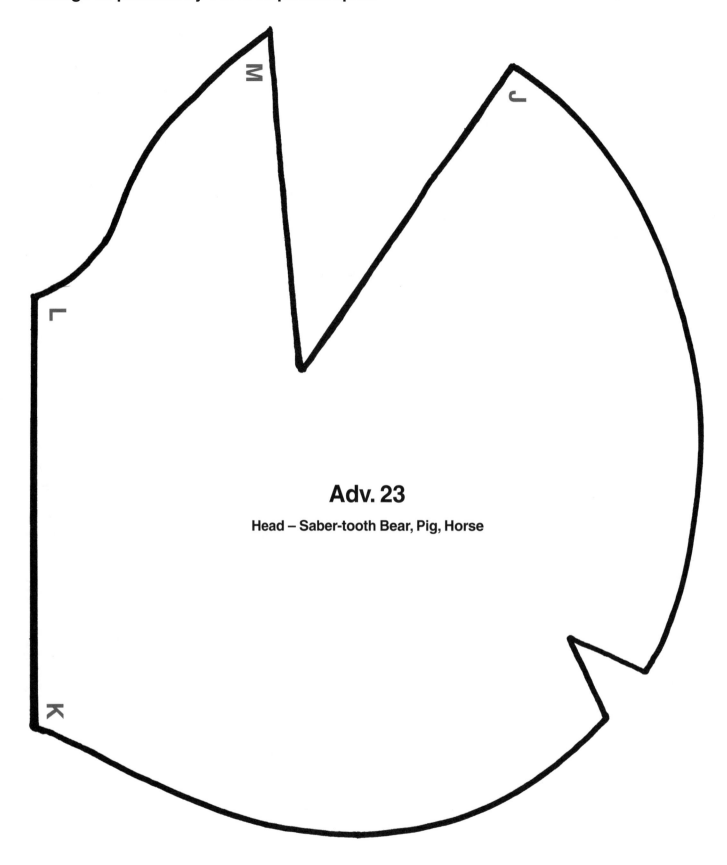

Adv. 23

Head – Saber-tooth Bear, Pig, Horse

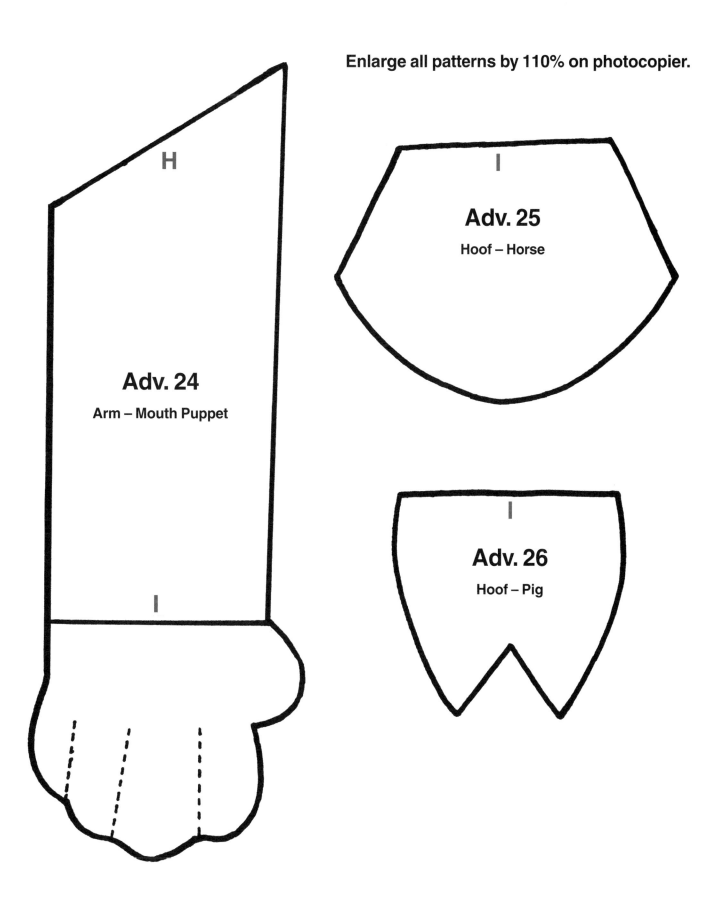

Enlarge all patterns by 110% on photocopier.

H

Adv. 24

Arm – Mouth Puppet

I

Adv. 25

Hoof – Horse

I

Adv. 26

Hoof – Pig

Enlarge all patterns by 110% on photocopier.

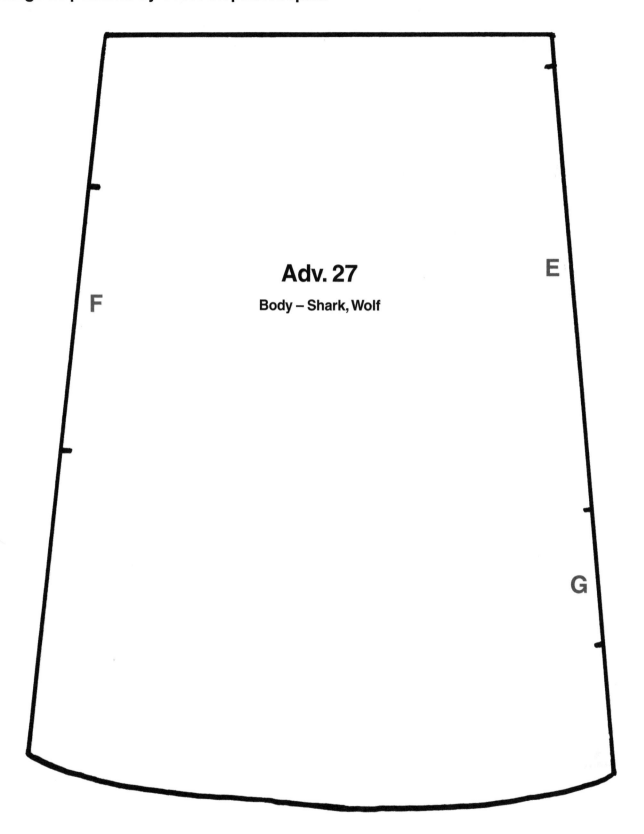

Adv. 27

Body – Shark, Wolf

F

E

G

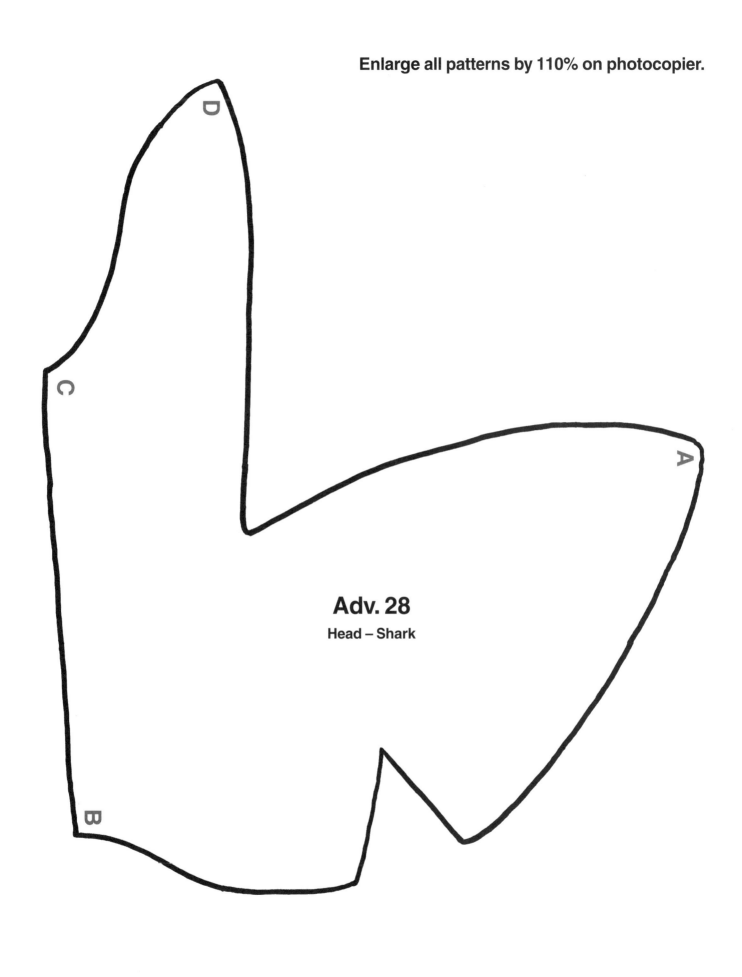

Adv. 28

Head – Shark

Enlarge all patterns by 110% on photocopier.

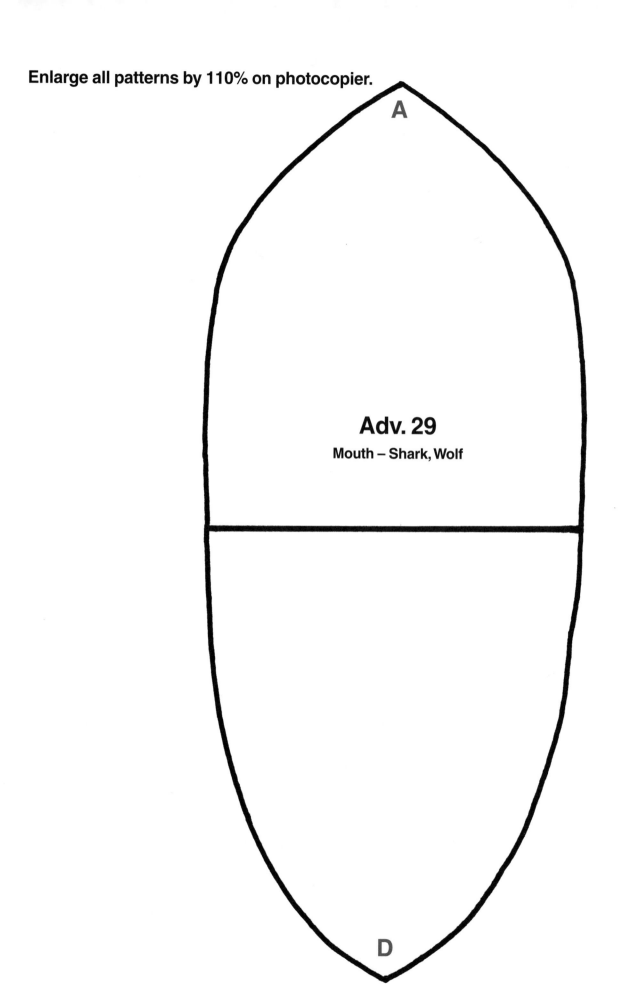

Adv. 29
Mouth – Shark, Wolf

Enlarge all patterns by 110% on photocopier.

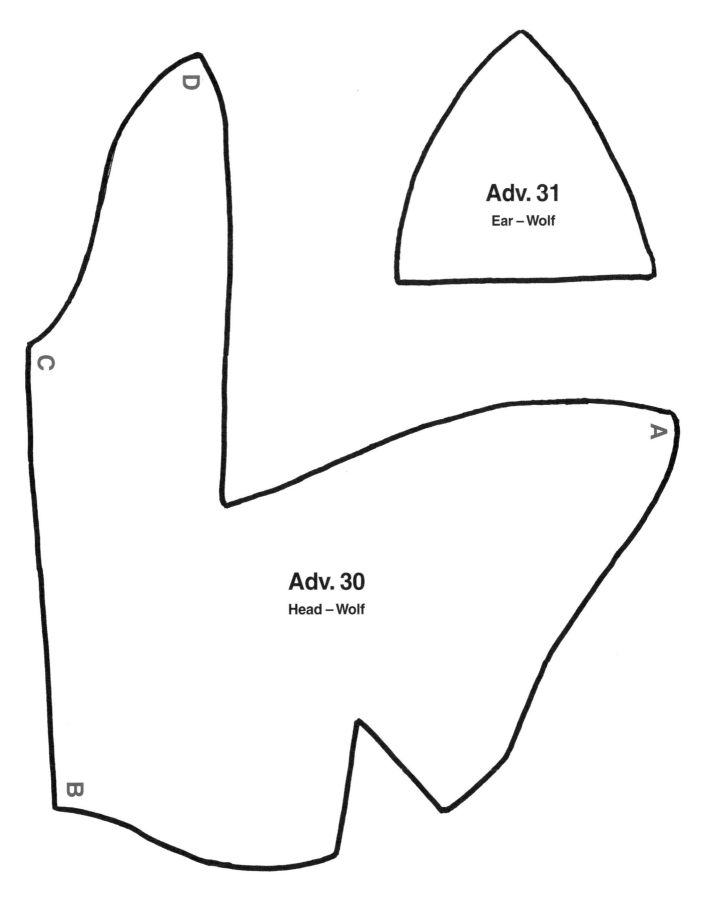

Adv. 31
Ear – Wolf

Adv. 30
Head – Wolf

Enlarge all patterns by 110% on photocopier.

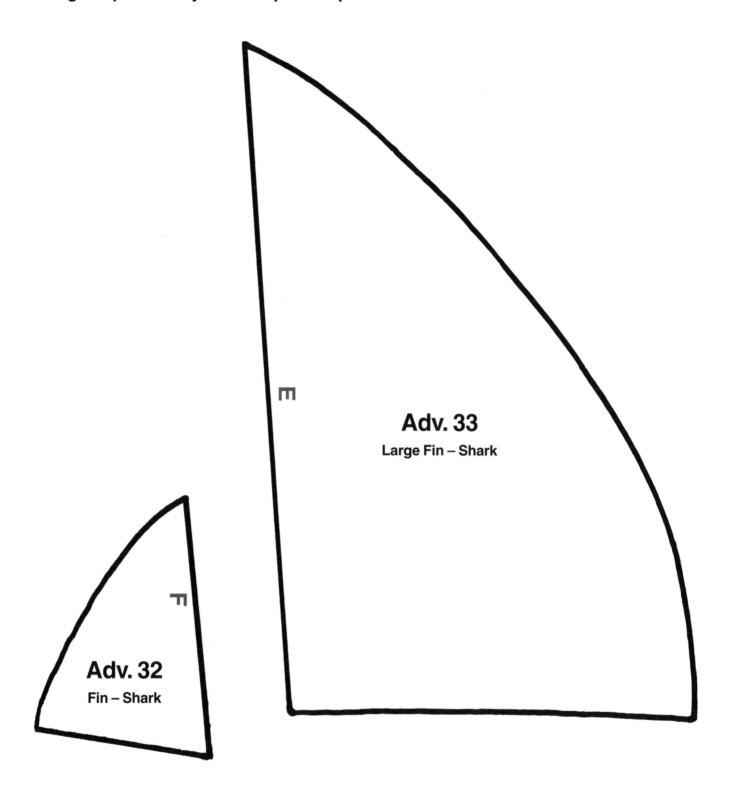

Adv. 33

Large Fin – Shark

Adv. 32

Fin – Shark

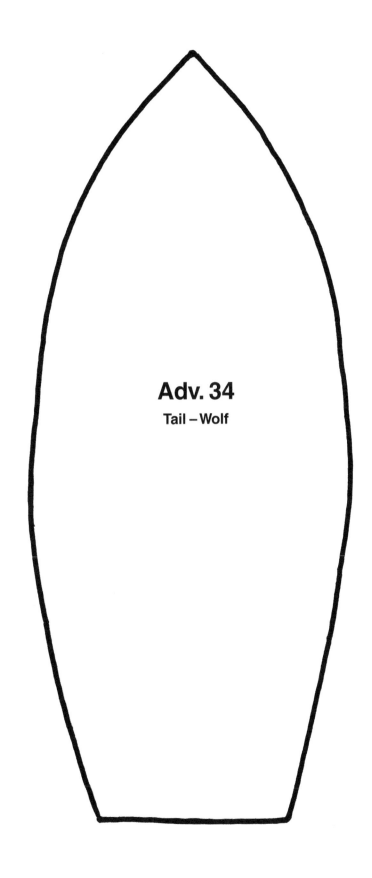

Adv. 34

Tail – Wolf

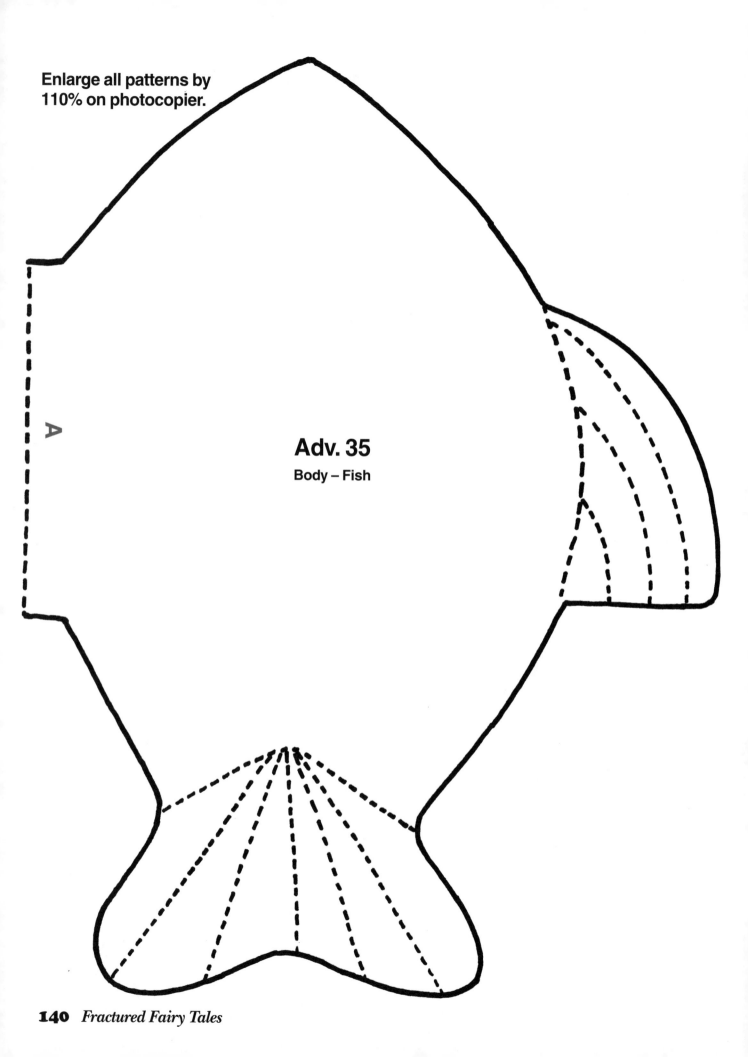

Enlarge all patterns by 110% on photocopier.

Adv. 35
Body – Fish

A

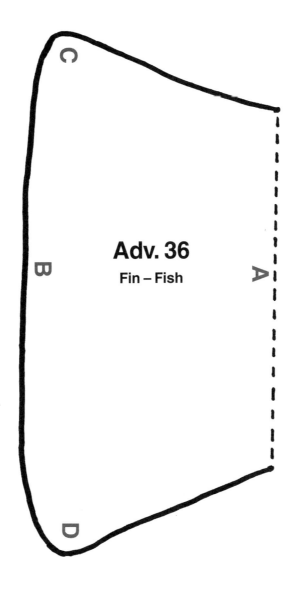

Adv. 36

Fin – Fish

Enlarge all patterns by 110% on photocopier.

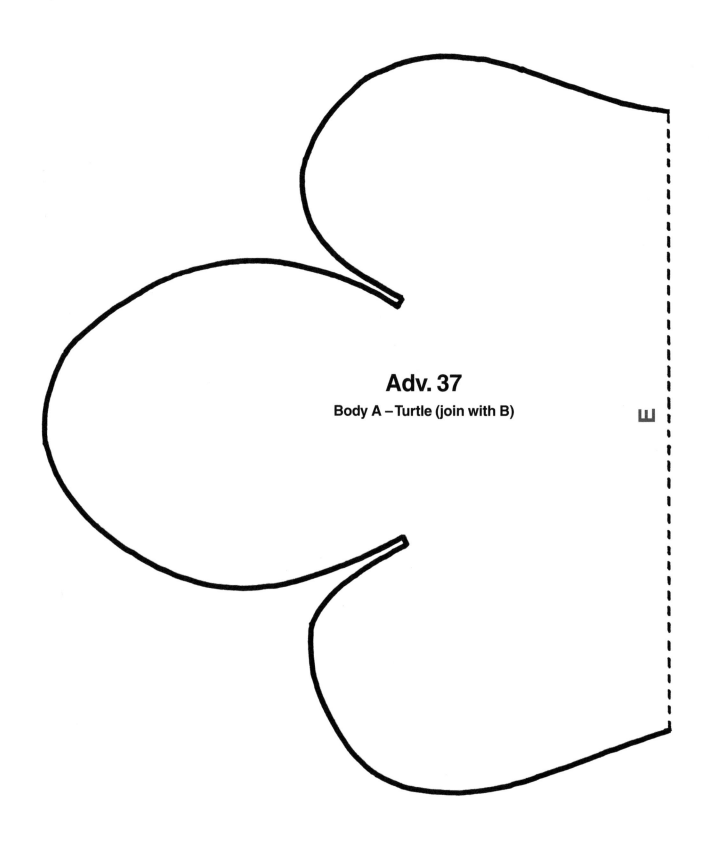

Adv. 37

Body A – Turtle (join with B)

E

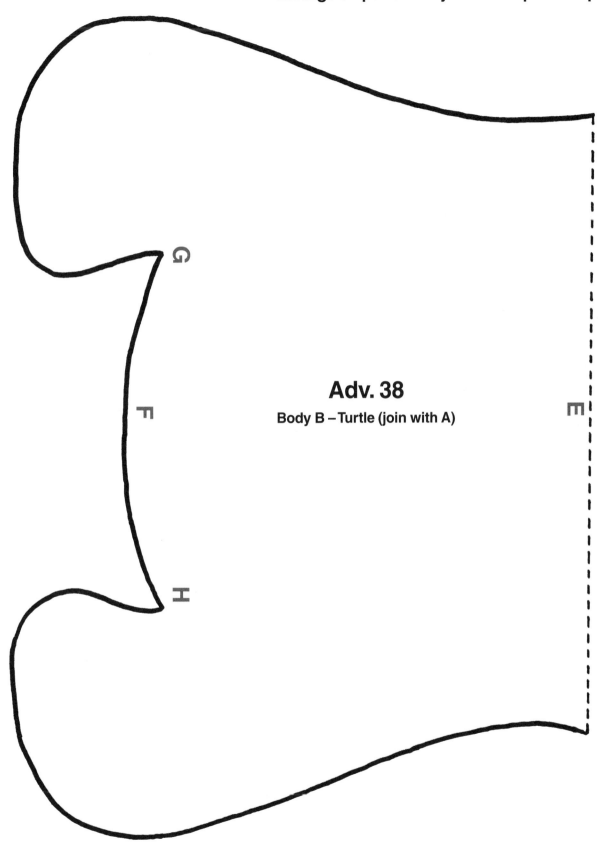

Adv. 38

Body B – Turtle (join with A)

G

F

E

H

Enlarge all patterns by 110% on photocopier.

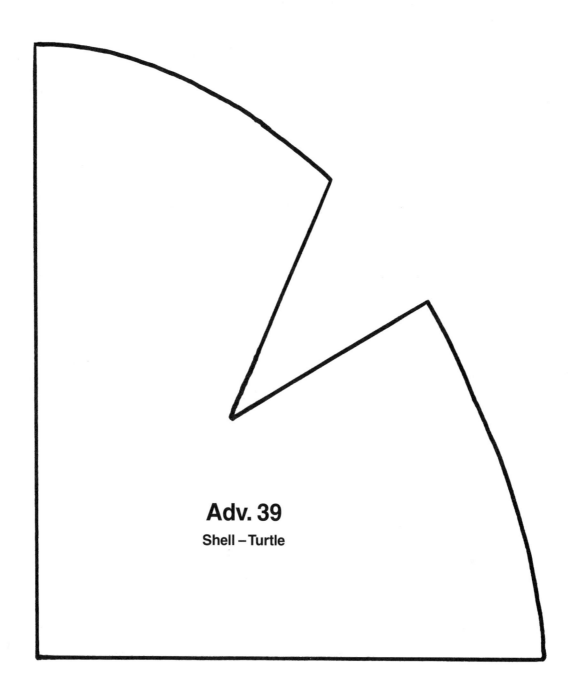

Adv. 39

Shell – Turtle

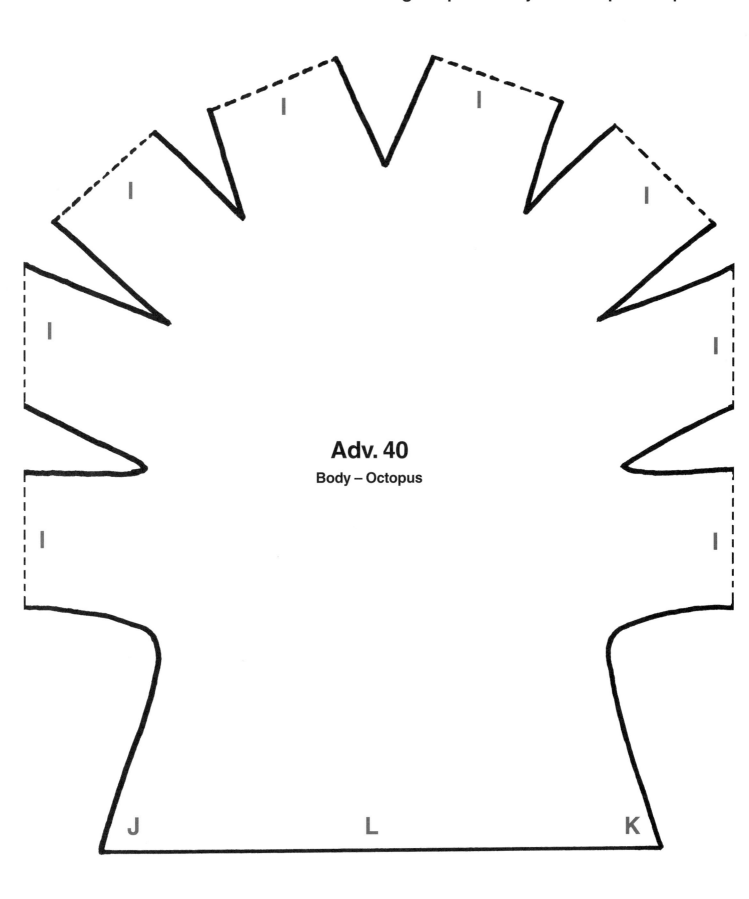

Adv. 40

Body – Octopus

J   L   K

Enlarge all patterns by 110% on photocopier.

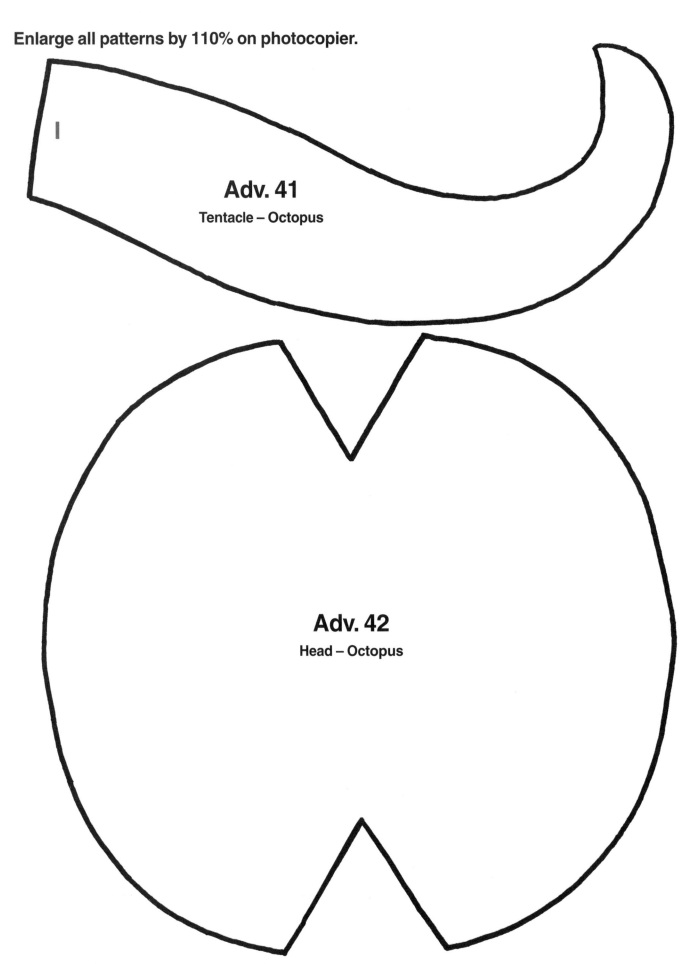

Adv. 41

Tentacle – Octopus

Adv. 42

Head – Octopus

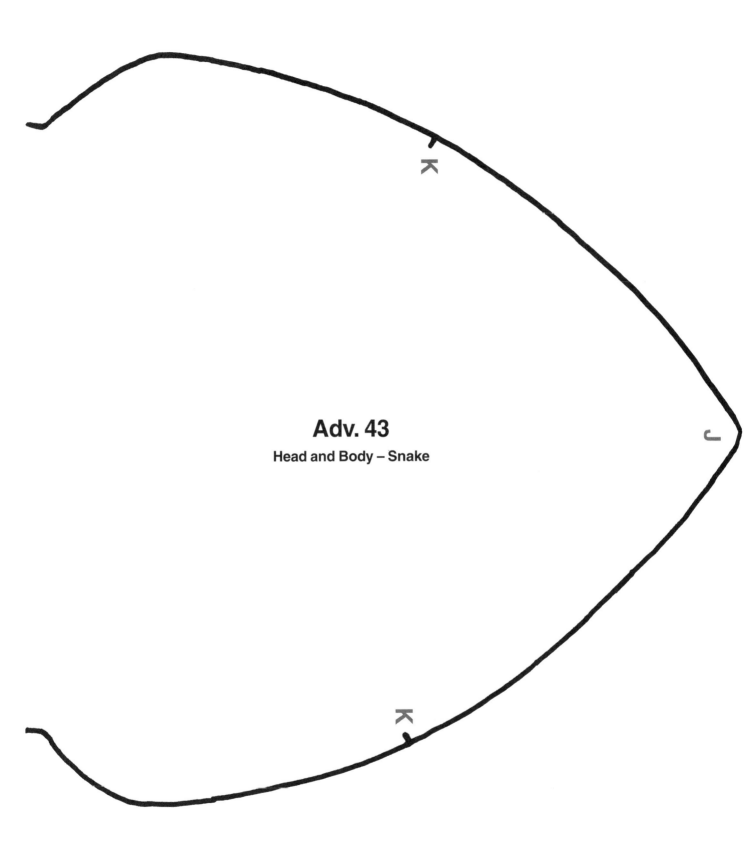

Adv. 43

Head and Body – Snake

Enlarge all patterns by 110% on photocopier.

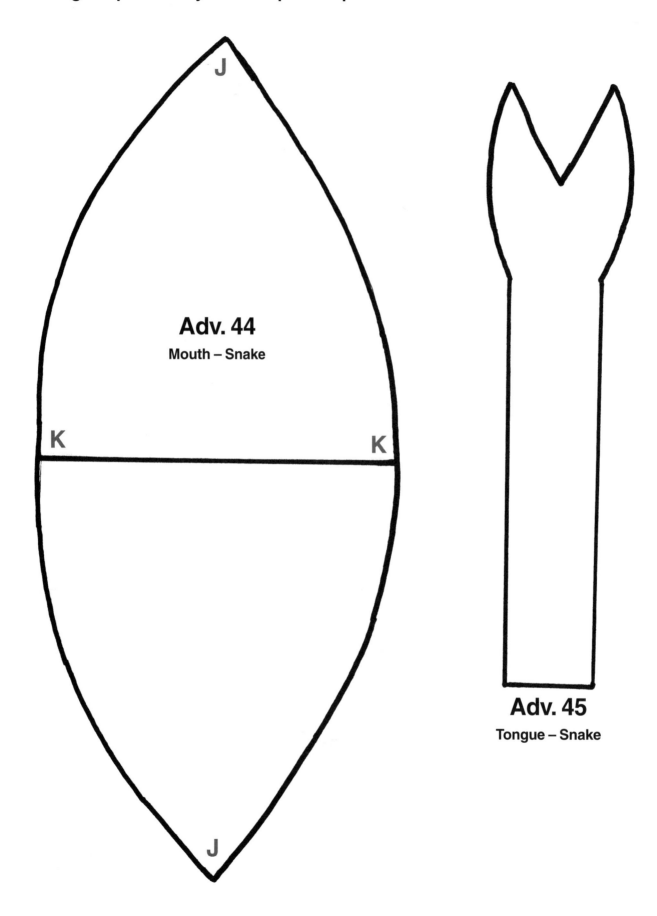

J

Adv. 44

Mouth – Snake

K   K

J

Adv. 45

Tongue – Snake

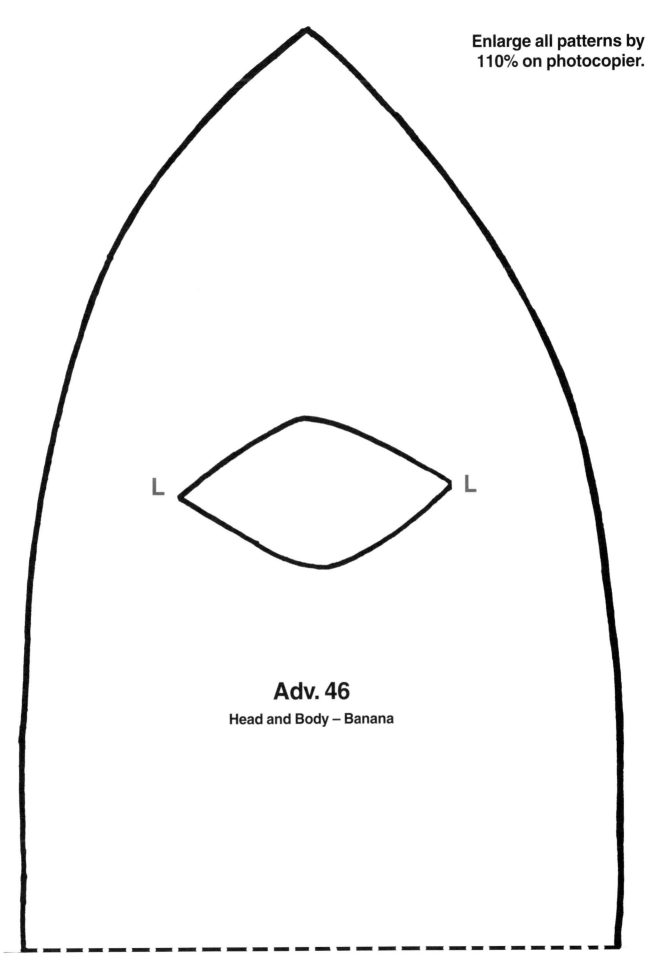

L   L

Adv. 46

Head and Body – Banana

Enlarge all patterns by 110% on photocopier.

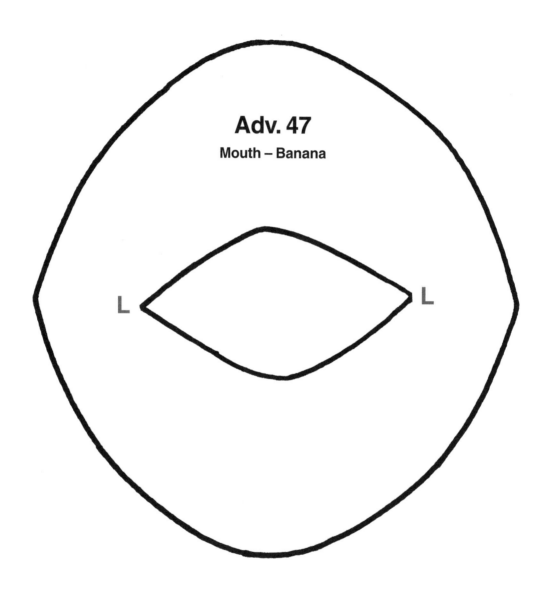

Adv. 47

Mouth – Banana

L

L

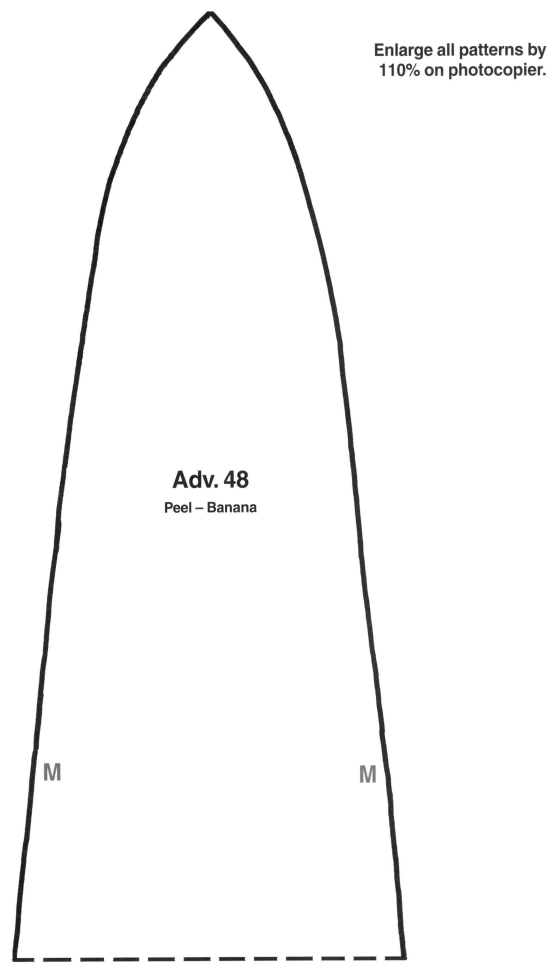

Enlarge all patterns by 110% on photocopier.

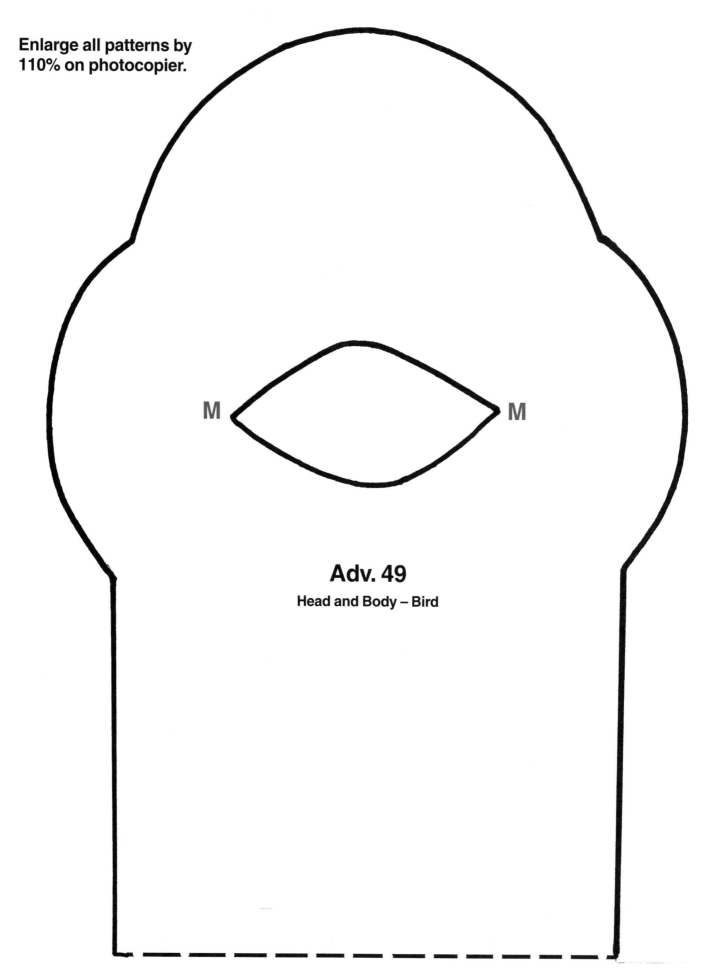

M   M

Adv. 49

Head and Body – Bird

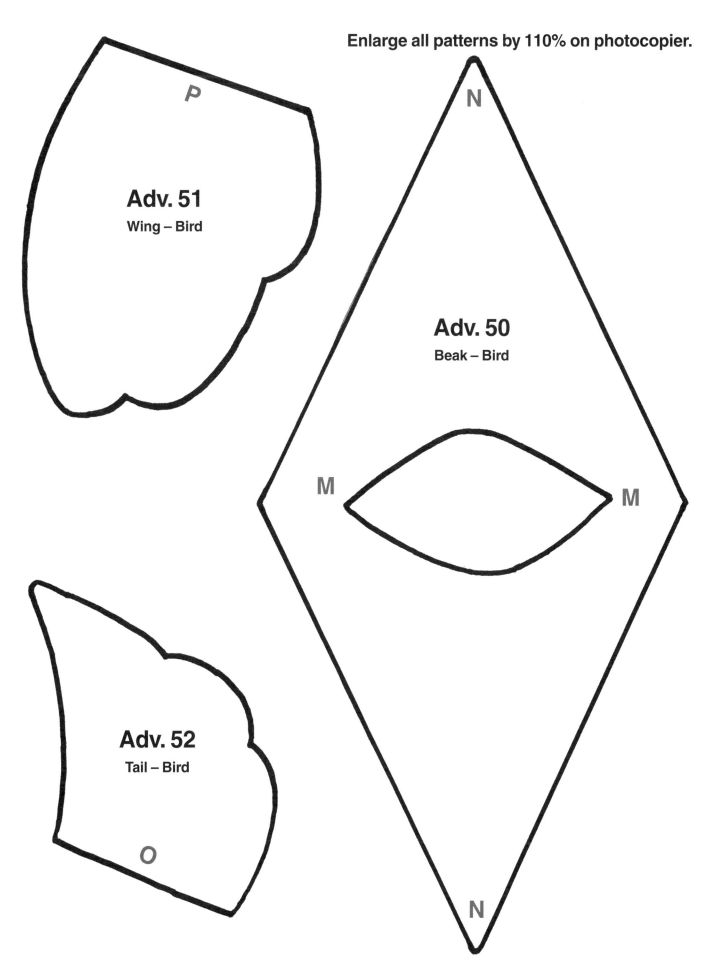

Enlarge all patterns by 110% on photocopier.

P

Adv. 51
Wing – Bird

N

Adv. 50
Beak – Bird

M   M

Adv. 52
Tail – Bird

O

N

Samples of Advanced Puppets

Little Green O'Glenn from "Little Green O'Glenn and the Lazy Leprechauns" (bird directions on pg. 122)

Snake from "Jungle Jack and the Vinestalk" (directions on pg. 121)

Banana from "Jungle Jack and the Vinestalk" (directions on pg. 121)

Miscellaneous Character (person mouth puppet directions on pg. 115)

Wolf from "Little Red Racing Heart" (directions on pg. 119)

Red Racing Heart from "Little Red Racing Heart" (person mouth puppet directions on pg. 115)

Jungle Jack and Mama from "Jungle Jack and the Vinestalk" (person mouth puppet directions on pg. 115)

Fish from "The Three Little Fishies and the Big, Bad Shark" (directions on pg. 120)

Pa and Ma Saber-tooth Bear from "Triceralocks and the Saber-tooth Bears" (directions on pg. 117)

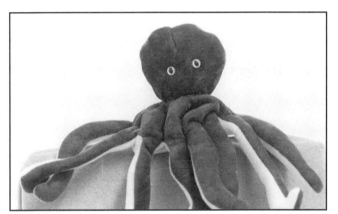

Octopus from "Triceralocks and the Saber-tooth Bears" (directions on pg. 121)

Tortoise and Hare from "Little Red Racing Heart" (turtle directions on pg. 120; rabbit directions on pg. 114)

Additional Resources on Puppetry and Storytelling

Anderson, Dee. *Amazingly Easy Puppet Plays: 42 New Scripts for One-Person Puppetry*. ALA, 1996. Short skits for one-person puppet plays.

Astell-Burt, Caroline. *I Am the Story: The Art of Puppetry in Education and Therapy*. Souvenir Press, 2002. An updated version of an earlier copy which demonstrates the use of puppetry in special projects for education and therapy.

Bauer, Caroline Feller. *New Handbook for Storytellers*. ALA, 1997. Contains a number of components on puppetry in storytelling and programming.

Creegan, George. *Sir George's Book of Hand Puppetry*. Follet Pub. Co., 1966.

Engler, Larry, and Carol Fijan. *Making Puppets Come Alive: How to Learn and Teach Hand Puppetry*. Dover, 1996. An easy-to-follow guide for voice use and synchronization, stage deportment and interactions, improvisation, staging, lighting, and much more. An excellent resource for puppet manipulation.

Henson, Cheryl. *The Muppets Make Puppets!: How to Make Puppets Out of All Kinds of Stuff Around Your House*. Workman Publishing Company, 1994. A kit containing instructions and materials to create imaginative puppets.

Jones, Taffy. *Old Barn Puppet Plays: Eight Plans for 10-Minute Puppetry Experiences for Children 5–8*. McFarland & Company, 1997. Easy-to-present puppet plays, and instructions on how to make Old Barn Theatres.

Lade, Roger. *The Most Excellent Book of How to Be a Puppeteer*. Millbrook Press, 1996. Patterns for 9 simple-to-make puppets.

Marks, Burton, and Rita Marks. *Puppet Plays and Puppet-Making*. Kalmbach Publishing, 1985.

Merton, George. *The Hand Puppets*. Thomas Nelson and Sons, 1957.

Minkel, Walter. *How to Do "The Three Bears" With Two Hands: Performing with Puppets*. ALA, 2000. Includes some traditional puppet plays for novice puppeteers.

Renfro, Nancy. *Puppet Shows Made Easy!* Nancy Renfro Studios, 1995.

Ross, Laura. *Hand Puppets: How to Make and Use Them*. Dover, 1990. A revision of a 1969 publication. Contains a light introduction into the history of puppetry, as well as directions and diagrams for making puppets, setting up a stage, and writing and producing your own show.

Smith, Thomasina. *Crafty Puppets (Crafty Kids)*. Gareth Stevens, 1999. Of interest to the teacher who is planning classroom puppet making.

VanSchuyver, Jan M. *Storytelling Made Easy with Puppets*. Oryx Press, 1993. A good introduction to using puppets in various types of programming.

Worrell, Estelle Ansley. *Be a Puppeteer! The Lively Puppet Book*. McGraw-Hill Book Co., 1969. Instructions for adapting plays as well as how to make puppets, costumes, sets, a stage, and all of the other equipment needed for a puppet theater.